RAILWAYS
IN THE
LANDSCAPE

RAILWAYS
IN THE
LANDSCAPE

How they transformed the face of Britain

by

GORDON BIDDLE

PEN & SWORD
TRANSPORT

COVER

FRONT
Great Western locomotive 6024 *King Edward* I takes the *Torbay Express* charter train along the South Devon coast at Dawlish. *2006*. Colin J. Marsden

BACK
Top: Preserved T9 locomotive 30120 and train on the Swanage Railway traversing the Dorset landscape near Corfe Castle. *2014*. Mike Esau
Middle: Connel Ferry Bridge which carried the Ballachulish branch over Loch Etive, Argyll. *2008*. W. Fawcett
Middle: Ingleborough (2375ft) overlooks a train approaching Ribblehead Viaduct on the Settle & Carlisle Railway. *2008*. J.R. Broughton
Bottom: Train at Starcross on the South Devon coast. *1981*. J.R. Broughton

ILLUSTRATIONS

Illustrations are by the author or from his collection, except where otherwise acknowledged.
Photographic imaging by John R. Broughton.

BY THE SAME AUTHOR

Victorian Stations
The Canals of North West England, with Charles Hadfield (2 vols)
The British Railway Station, with Jeoffry Spence
Pennine Waterway: a Pictorial History of the Leeds & Liverpool Canal
Railway Stations in the North West
Lancashire Waterways
The Railway Heritage of Britain, with O.S. Nock
Great Railway Stations of Britain: their Architecture, Growth and Development
Railways around Preston: an Historical Review
The Railway Surveyors
The Oxford Companion to British Railway History, with Jack Simmons (eds)
Britain's Historic Railway Buildings: a Gazetteer of Structures and Sites

To Dorothy

First published in Great Britain in 2016 by
Pen & Sword Transport
An imprint of Pen & Sword Books Ltd
47 Church Street, Barnsley, South Yorkshire S70 2AS

ISBN 978 1 47386 2 357

Pen & Sword Books Ltd incorporates the imprints of Pen & Sword
Archaeology, Atlas, Aviation, Battleground, Discovery, Family History,
History, Maritime, Military, Naval, Politics, Railways, Select, Social History,
Transport, True Crime, and Claymore Press, Frontline Books, Leo Cooper,
Praetorian Press, Remember When, Seaforth Publishing and Wharncliffe.

For a complete list of Pen & Sword titles please contact
Pen & Sword Books Limited
47 Church Street, Barnsley, South Yorkshire S70 2AS England
E-mail: enquiries@pen-and-sword.co.uk
Website: www.pen-and-sword.co.uk

Printed and bound in India by Replika Press Pvt. Ltd

CONTENTS

HISTORICAL NOTE

Until 1923 there were over 120 separate railway companies in Britain, many themselves the result of earlier amalgamations and acquisitions. Under the 1921 Railways Act they were grouped into four big companies, the London Midland & Scottish (LMS), the London & North Eastern (LNER), an enlarged Great Western (GWR) and the Southern (SR). In 1948 these were nationalised as a single state-owned corporation, British Railways (BR). In 1994 under privatisation legislation, track and trains were separated. The infrastructure was placed under what eventually became the Government-owned Network Rail, while passenger train services were franchised to a number of private companies, partly on a regional basis. Freight trains operate under individual track access agreements.

PREFACE

The Industrial Revolution transformed the face of Britain, a process in which railways played a leading part, changing the economy and way of life. Much has been written about what the railways were, how they were built and operated, but less about what they did in creating a visual transformation of the countryside, towns and cities. It is hoped, therefore, that this book will appeal not only to readers interested in railways, but to a wider audience.

In rural areas we take railways for granted as part of the scene; in urban and industrial areas their impact is more emphatic, often obtrusive, but of necessity long accepted. Yet as long ago as 1955 W.G. Hoskins, in his seminal study *The Making of the English Landscape*, writing mainly about the rural scene, stated that the railways' impact was massive in the way that, to use his words, 'they manipulated the landscape on a grand scale.' That, of course, was before new dual carriageway roads and motorways began carving their way through towns and countryside. Even so, by comparison the overall damage has been more limited, whereas the railways went everywhere. Indeed, by 1901 railways controlled some 240,000 acres of land, or 11-12 acres per mile, in total half the size of Oxfordshire. Jack Simmons's *The Railway in Town and Country* (1986) is the only work to cover the subject comprehensively, especially in terms of the economy and communities, while in *The Victorian Railway* (1991) his chapters on 'Structures' and 'Loss and Gain' together form an admirably concise introduction to railway buildings. In *Railways in the British Isles: Landscape, Land Use and Society* (1982) David Turnock's three themes are the historical development of railways, their economic and social significance, and the contemporary scene at the time of writing. John R. Kellett's masterly *The Impact of Railways on Victorian Cities* (1969) concentrates on the largest towns, including a detailed examination of five. Jack Simmons's chapter 'The Power of the Railway' in *The Victorian City: Images and Realities*, Volume II, edited by H.J. Dyos and Michael Wolff (1973), discusses the same topic in a wider context. Several general studies have dwelt on the way in which railways transformed towns, but mostly in social and economic terms. More recently the eight-volume regional series *England's Landscapes* (2006) provides valuable overviews of railways in rural and urban settings. In volume 3, *The South West*, Roger Kain underlines Hoskins' statement fifty years earlier in saying that railways 'arguably brought the most profound landscape changes ever experienced.' But one of the most perceptive commentaries, although short, was made as long ago as 1962 by Michael Robbins in the chapter entitled 'Railways and the Landscape' in his book *The Railway Age*. Then in 2015 Robert Duck's *On the Edge* appeared just before this book went to the publisher: a specific work devoted, as the punning subtitle *Coastlines of Britain* indicates, to the effect of railways on Britain's coasts, in strictly geophysical terms that, despite occasionally being a little subjective, give much food for thought. Otherwise, in more recent years, apart from some academic works, little has been written that embraces all these themes to present a cohesive account of the visual transformations created by railways in town and country, both directly and indirectly.

Until the early 1900s the history of Britain's railways was one of continuous expansion, territorially and from internal growth, followed by a relatively static half-century until contraction began in the 1950s. Now, in the twenty-first century, they are expanding again,bringing more changes in the landscape.

Gordon Biddle
Summer, 2015

Chapter 1

TRANSFORMING THE RURAL SCENE

Among the many changes that over the centuries have contributed in transforming the English medieval landscape of moorland, forests and open land, farmed on a communal system, to the familiar one of today, three stand out as the most significant. The first two occurred slowly and more or less simultaneously over some 250 years from the time of the Tudors. As society became more settled and peaceful, moving into what has been called the Age of Enlightenment, the great landowners began a process of reshaping the landscape by improving their land, planting trees and woodland, introducing more productive farming methods and enhancing their estates by building themselves grand new houses in large, newly-created areas of parkland. It was an age which produced skilled landscape architects like Humphry Repton, William Kent, Lancelot 'Capability' Brown and, in the early nineteenth century, Joseph Paxton who later achieved fame as the designer of the Crystal Palace for the Great Exhibition of 1851.They and their employers believed that they were not only 'taming nature' but improving on it; not a new concept, but one that went back to the ancient civilisations of Egypt, Greece and Rome. At the same time, more efficient farming gradually spread to lesser landholdings, combining to completely alter the character of the countryside. This could only be carried through by the second great change, the enclosure of open land to form fields and farmsteads, particularly in lowland areas. In England and parts of Wales it began slowly in the seventeenth century, either by agreement between landowner and tenant or, more often, by compulsion, then speeding up as it was increasingly enforced by legislation. Between 1760 and 1850 Parliament approved over 2,000 private Enclosure Acts. In Scotland's agricultural lowlands, which had their own system of land tenure, the process began later, but was completed at about the same time. Changes in the sparsely populated Highlands, which had a completely different economic and social order, were political in origin following the 1745 Jacobite Rebellion; country dominated by the mountainous terrain.

In direct contrast, the third great change was extraordinarily rapid. It was brought about by the invention of the steam railway, which in less than seventy years grew into a comprehensive network, second in the world in density only to Belgium's, so that by 1900 few places in Britain, excepting the Scottish Highlands, were more than 5 miles from a railway station. By the time the first main line railway as we know it was opened between Liverpool and Manchester in 1830, significant parts of Britain during the previous three quarters of a century had already been steadily changing from an agrarian to an industrial society in areas like the Staffordshire Black Country and the Potteries, north-east England, the textile districts of Lancashire and Yorkshire, South Wales and central Scotland. There, steam power had introduced industrialisation, yet elsewhere outside large cities the landscape essentially was still rural, with pockets of small-scale manufacturing relying on hand, horse, wind and water power.

The eighteenth-century turnpike roads and later new roads improved travel, having some economic effect by speeding up communications, but comparatively little visually; it would be 150 years before tarmac highways spread across the land. Industrial growth was centred on areas served by navigable rivers and canals, a system begun in earnest in 1760, and by 1830 almost complete. In country areas the impact of canals on the landscape was largely benign as they twisted and turned along the contours of the land, their rounded hump-backed bridges, shallow cuttings and low embankments, broken here and there by locks and the occasional aqueduct, blending gently into the rural scene. In towns it was less so, their passage attracting industry and often creating squalor, although most canal buildings themselves were quite seemly. Before and during the canal era, short, primitive horse-operated railways using wooden or iron rails, called tramroads or wagonways, were built, usually to connect mines and quarries to navigable waterways. Because they tended to avoid heavy earthworks, in general they left fewer permanent marks on the landscape, although in north-east England and South Wales, where a lot of colliery tramroads were built, a number of prominent remains can still be seen, for example the celebrated Causey Arch, 130ft wide and 80ft high, and a 100ft high embankment, both on the Tanfield wagonway in County Durham, completed in 1727; and the curving line of Hill's Tramroad of 1815-25 around Blorenge Mountain near Blaenavon in Gwent, which includes a tunnel. Both sites are scheduled Ancient Monuments. They make prominent features in some other parts of the country, too, such as at Ticknall, in south Derbyshire, where a stone arch over the village street carried a tramroad of the same name, and the Poldice tramroad in Cornwall, most of it now a footpath.

The effect of railways was totally different from that of canals. It was explosive. Whereas inland navigation of some 4,000 miles took eighty-odd years to complete, the same mileage of railways was built in five. By the end of the nineteenth century it exceeded 18,000. Such unprecedented expansion was enormously disruptive. For instance, it has been estimated that between 1830 and 1850 the railways built over 25,000 bridges, more than twice the number that had existed before. But the physical disruption, although great, was relatively short-lived as life adjusted to the new means of locomotion and travel. The greater change lay in the speeding up of industrial growth by providing fast and easy transport, not only of raw materials and finished goods, but of workers migrating from the countryside to the new factories in

The Tappendens' Tramroad, built in 1805, connected their Abernant Ironworks to the Aberdare Canal in South Wales. Parts are traceable, some with stone sleeper blocks still visible. *2005.*

the fast-expanding towns. The process that began in the canal age was now hugely accelerated. The canals themselves entered a period of gradual decline, while by the 1850s most turnpikes had been relegated to local parish supervision.

Railway routes

The effect of railways on the landscape was a two-way process. The land itself dictated the course a railway could take, and where natural obstacles like hills and rivers intervened, the railway could either go round, tunnel through, or build a bridge or viaduct as the case might be. Conversely, in doing so the railway in turn changed the landscape, sometimes unobtrusively, often dramatically, infinitely more than its predecessors, the turnpike roads and the canals, although they too had been strongly influenced by topography, taking natural routes that to a large extent the early railways followed. As an example, the London & Birmingham Railway from London northward to Northamptonshire roughly followed the course of the Roman Watling Street, which Thomas Telford improved to form the Holyhead Road, and the Grand Junction Canal, while the Great Northern Railway from London to Doncaster did not stray very far from the Great North Road. In hilly and mountainous terrains there was no choice but to follow the valleys as far as possible. Both of the trans-Pennine routes between Manchester and Leeds keep close to river, road and canal. The Highland Railway through the Grampians from Dunkeld to Daviot, on the route to Inverness of 1863, closely follows Telford's road, which itself more or less keeps to General Wade's military road of 1734. In the flat fenland country of Lincolnshire three railways followed straightened rivers and drainage dykes, the longest for 25 miles along the banks of the River Witham and the South Forty Foot Drain between Lincoln and Boston. From Thorne almost to Scunthorpe the railway followed a long section of the Stainforth & Keadby Canal. In Cornwall part of the Liskeard & Looe Railway was built on a canal, and most of the Glasgow Paisley & Johnstone Canal was converted into a railway. But in general these were exceptional. Although a good number of

canals were taken over by railways to eliminate competition, usually they were too winding to accommodate the track.

Unlike canals, railways by their nature had to take the most direct route, avoiding sharp curves. In doing so they ruthlessly cut across field patterns, some not long created, dividing land holdings. To quote from Christian Barman's *Early British Railways*, 'When the straight new roads [i.e. railways] were laid across fields they slashed like a knife through the delicate tissue of settled rural civilisation.' In his contemporary account of a journey on the London & Birmingham Railway, Charles Dickens was typically eloquent in *Dombey and Son* when he described it as 'defiant of all paths and roads, piercing the heart of every obstacle….through the clay, through the rock.' A glance at a large-scale Ordnance Survey map of lowland areas will show small, irregularly-shaped fields cut off by the railway from larger fields on the opposite side of the line. That is why British railways have so many accommodation bridges and crossings, so-called

Trans-Pennine canal and railway share the narrow Calder Valley near Todmorden. *1976.*

because they were provided – often reluctantly – to accommodate landowners by connecting their severed lands. Occupation bridges and crossings served the same purpose on private roads and tracks. Severance also divided communities and parishes, creating areas that were literally 'the wrong side of the tracks', just as new roads and motorways have done today.

In crossing public highways, railway companies had to provide a bridge, adding to the cost, or, where levels were suitable, a level crossing, always much cheaper but often creating the continuing expense of manning. There were numerous instances of a landowner, parish or turnpike trust insisting on a bridge where a level crossing would have sufficed, imposing on the railway the additional cost of raising or lowering the road. Where a projected railway crossed a road at an acute angle, often it was cheaper to divert the road on to a double bend so that a bridge could be built at right angles to the tracks, saving the considerable extra expense of a skewed arch.

Similarly, in order to keep a straight course, sometimes it was cheaper to straighten out a meandering river instead of building bridges over loops, as happened in the shallow Calder Valley in West Yorkshire between Wakefield and Normanton, and for

A zig-zag bridge over the railway at Keer Holme near Carnforth, showing how the road was diverted to cross the railway perpendicularly instead of on a skew arch, which would have been much more expensive to construct. The road can be seen rejoining its original course beyond the bridge. *2012.*

⅔ mile of the River Yare at Norwich. Canalised sections of the River Don Navigation near Rotherham were diverted on to less convenient artificial cuts so that the Manchester, Sheffield & Lincolnshire Railway could use the older, straighter channels. The line from Oxford to Birmingham diverted the River Cherwell in Oxfordshire for nearly ½ mile near Heyford, and on the Oxford–Worcester line a similar length of the Evenlode near Combe was moved. Narrow valleys forced railways to keep more closely to the contours, often needing sharp curves and numerous bridges. The Esk Valley in North Yorkshire, for instance, crosses the tortuous river seventeen times in the 14½ miles from Lealholme to Whitby, while in Cumbria the line through the Greta gorge east of Keswick criss-crossed the river on eight ugly bowstring girder bridges in little over 3 miles. In South Devon the Kingsbridge branch wriggled down the valley of the River Avon from the main line at Brent, crossing the river eight times in the 7 miles from Avonwick to Loddiswell. In south-west Scotland the Glasgow, Dumfries & Carlisle Railway is superbly engineered for 8 miles down narrow, winding Nithsdale south of Sanquhar, needing three viaducts and the impressive Priestwood embankment, high on a tall retaining wall, before it swings away to tunnel through a spur of the Lowther Hills, and that only to comply with the wishes of the Duke of Buccleugh who didn't want the railway near his seat at Drumlanrig Castle. Away to the north beyond Perth, the Highland Railway only managed to squeeze through the Pass of Killiecrankie by means of making a shelf on a high retaining wall, followed by an unusual viaduct of ten arches built lengthwise along the side of the gorge and, finally, a tunnel.

The Duke of Buccleugh's demand was just one of many human-inspired obstacles added to the natural ones encountered by railway engineers. Many landowners successfully objected to railways crossing their estates, insisting on diversions or, like the duke, a tunnel to keep the line out of sight. The Earl of Essex forced the London & Birmingham Railway to make a diversion and a mile-long tunnel at Watford to avoid Cassiobury Park, which had been laid out by Humphry Repton; Marley Tunnel in Devon was built solely to keep the South Devon Railway out of Lord Carew's view from Syon Abbey. Best known was 'Lord Harborough's Curve' around Stapleford Park at Saxby, Leicestershire, which had been landscaped by Capability Brown. For over forty years the sharp curve slowed down Midland Railway trains until an easier alignment was permitted in 1892. Not a few landowners exercised double standards by successfully objecting to a railway crossing their land while profitably investing in others.

Not only private interests prevailed on railway routes; the state, too, could be equally awkward, as when the Commissioners of Woods and Forests compelled the Southampton & Dorchester Railway to take a winding route through Crown property in the New Forest. Then, as time went by, and landowners began to realise that a railway could enhance the value of their property, their attitudes changed to one of welcome, many of them actively encouraging the building of secondary routes and branch lines to fill gaps in the network. In 1864 the value of railways was recognised in the Improvement of Land Act that allowed landowners to charge investment in railways to their estates.

Railway construction caused tremendous upheavals in local life as contractors and their itinerant workers moved in, not only digging and building on an unprecedented scale but on lesser works such as laying temporary roads across fields where there was no other convenient access. Yet once the navvies, masons and bricklayers had gone and the new railways' scars had healed, cuttings and embankments grown over and trees and bushes established, even the deepest and highest earthworks were steadily absorbed into the landscape, a process aided by turfing and seeding to assist them to stabilise, leaving nothing like the broad scars of modern dual carriageway highways and motorways. Tring Cutting, on the London & Birmingham Railway, is 2½ miles long and 70ft deep; Cowran Hills Cutting on the Newcastle & Carlisle Railway, is almost a mile long and 110ft deep

Osborne's London and Birmingham Railway Guide, published in 1840, two years after the line opened throughout, described the banks of Oxhey Cutting near Watford as 'beautiful gardens of wild flowers.' Wherever possible the spoil from cuttings was

used to form embankments but if there was insufficient, recourse might be made to digging soil from what are known as side-pits in adjoining fields, many of which remain today. Some became lakes. Gravel for track ballast was obtained in the same way, and the results can be seen on the Great Western south of Oxford and on the Hull & Holderness Railway near Hedon. Eventually the railways' passage through the landscape came to be marked more by prominent post-and-rail fencing, endless miles of telegraph poles and wires, and intermittent tall semaphore signals. Otherwise, the main intrusions were bridges, viaducts, tunnels and, to a lesser degree, stations and lineside buildings. In unpopulated mountainous and moorland areas, railways were almost totally absorbed in broad, unbroken landscapes, marked only by viaducts where they crossed valleys.

By the 1830s, for nearly a century there had been an active and increasing appreciation of natural beauty and a taste for the picturesque, natural and man-made. Consequently, in many quarters railway building was viewed with widespread alarm. Condemnation was voiced by leading figures such as William Wordsworth and John Ruskin, although in time even they had

Cowran Hills Cutting, nearly a mile long and 110ft deep, on the Newcastle & Carlisle Railway near Brampton. *2015*.

to acknowledge that there were instances where railways did, in fact, set off natural beauty. Moreover, railways allowed a far wider enjoyment of unspoiled landscapes by bringing them within easy reach of the population at large. Consequently, for the first twenty-five years or so railway structures were built in a seemly, tasteful manner that respected their surroundings or, in some contemporary eyes, even improved them, especially by using local traditional materials. Then, after about 1856, the railways themselves introduced alien materials by providing cheap, easy transport countrywide, slowly swamping traditional ways of building with mass-produced bricks, roofing slates and iron ware where hitherto they had been unknown.

Rural bridges and viaducts

The most prominent features of the railway in the countryside are its bridges and viaducts. Bridges built in the first thirty years or so were arched; either semi-circular, segmental or, less frequently, semi-elliptical, constructed in local stone or brick according to locality, or occasionally iron. Often, suitable stone or clay for brickmaking was found when digging cuttings. Once they had weathered, their rounded outlines helped to mould them into their surroundings.

Like their forebears the canal builders, the early railway engineers were imbued with a sense of place and proportion that derived from an age of elegance; one that soon was to end. They were inspired by a combination of the eighteenth-century spirit of romanticism and a powerful recognition that they were achieving something on a scale hitherto without parallel that would revolutionise society. To them and, especially, their directors who held the purse strings, railways were more than just a new source of profit. They were the symbol of a new age. Consequently, with the supreme self-confidence that characterised the Victorians, they deliberately set out to make their viaducts impressive, giving them an air of powerful grandeur and, often, sheer elegance; in spirit emulating the great arched Roman aqueducts of southern Europe. If intrusion on the landscape could not be avoided, they would instead try to enhance it by embellishing the rural scene, thereby combining the aesthetically acceptable with the functional, a popular view that was readily accepted and admired by contemporary observers.

Viaducts frequently were subjects for illustrating enthusiastic descriptions in early railway guidebooks. Isaac Shaw's *Views on the line of the Liverpool and Manchester Railway* of 1831 calls the Sankey viaduct a 'beautiful structure' and extols the views from trains passing over it. *Drake's Road Book of the Grand Junction Railway*, published in 1838, says of the Dutton Viaduct over the River Weaver in Cheshire 'This gigantic structure exceeds in magnitude anything of the kind yet accomplished in this country, perhaps in Europe, not even excepting the Menai Bridge [Telford's].The grandeur of this stupendous work is greatly enhanced by the richness and beauty of the adjacent country.' Even in 1883, when great viaducts no longer excited the sense of awe and wonder of earlier years, F.S. Williams in *Our Iron Roads* felt inspired to write of Chirk Viaduct on the Shrewsbury & Chester Railway, built in 1848, 'The boldness of its style and the chasteness of its finish are exceedingly effective. Such architecture imparts grace and beauty… Viewed from beneath the vast structure presents a noble appearance.' It was a concept that soon was lost but has been revived today. John Ruskin detested railways and was vociferous in his condemnation of the railway through his beloved Peak District, particularly in Monsal Dale, calling it 'close-clinging damnation', although it didn't stop him from using it. Yet when British Railways proposed to demolish Monsal Dale Viaduct after the line closed in 1968 there was an outcry from conservationists. The viaduct no longer violated; it was now considered to be an integral part of the landscape. Nowhere have viaducts become so totally assimilated into the landscape as on the Settle & Carlisle Railway, all twenty-one of them, as much a part of the Pennine moorlands as the drystone walls.

Viaducts vary greatly in character as well as in size. The slender elegance of Robert Stephensons's twenty-eight tall semi-circular masonry arches of the Royal Border Bridge of 1850 at Berwick, 120ft high, in their simplicity perfectly complement the shallow valley of the Tweed. Conversely, the nineteen even

taller arches of Leaderfoot Viaduct of 1865, further upstream where the valley is narrow, are equally complementary. The thirty-one creamy stone arches of Crimple Viaduct, near Harrogate, 110ft high, form a dramatic backdrop in a broad, open valley. Harringworth Viaduct of 1879, although only 58ft high, is no less dramatic for its great length of nearly ¾ mile, the longest in Britain, as it crosses the broad Welland Valley in Northamptonshire. Unfortunately the original red bricks made from nearby clay deposits proved to be of poor quality, requiring extensive replacement over the years with more durable blue engineering bricks, resulting in a patchy appearance with more blue than red. Time has been kinder to Scotland's longest viaduct, Culloden Moor (1898) south of Inverness. Twenty-eight red sandstone arches, 132ft high, with a broad central arch across the River Nairn, have a certain dour beauty as they stride purposefully across the open moorland. The value of these and others like them in wide landscapes lies in their spare, clean lines and lack of adornment.

I.K. Brunel built a number of graceful semi-elliptical arched bridges on the original Great Western Railway of 1838-41, notably the Wharncliffe Viaduct at Hanwell. 'Few viaducts have such architectural panache' wrote Nikolaus Pevsner in the *London, North West* volume in his *Buildings of England* series, a compliment that can be equally applied to Brunel's Maidenhead Bridge across the Thames. When the Wharncliffe Viaduct was widened to take four tracks in 1872, great care was taken to match the new with the old. The same care was exercised with Charles Vignoles' Ribble Bridge at Preston when it was widened in 1880, only to have the downstream side disfigured by ugly latticed steel spans for a second widening in 1904. The Ouse Valley Viaduct at Balcombe, on the London & Brighton Railway in East Sussex, crossing a valley that is narrow and partly wooded, carries adornments that, in the right place, add to the scene. Pevsner considered it to be one of the most impressive in England. Others have called it the most elegant in Britain. Completed in 1841, it has thirty-seven semi-circular red brick arches 96ft high, embellished in classical style with delicately balustraded parapets terminating at each end with two ornamental Italianate pavilions, all in specially imported Caen stone; an outstanding example of the confidence and vision of the early railway builders.

The prize for sheer unadorned grace goes to two bridges: the delicately proportioned Ballochmyle Viaduct in Ayrshire (1845), and the Victoria Bridge across the Wear at Penshaw, Tyne & Wear (1838). Ballochmyle's 181ft central arch was for fifty years the world's second widest masonry arch, exceeded only by the Grosvenor Bridge at Chester of 1834. In local pink sandstone with deep red dressings, it crosses the River Ayr in a narrow wooded valley which, unfortunately, is not too easily accessible. The Victoria Bridge, however, is easily seen from a riverside path. Four unequal arches spanning from 100ft to 160ft have particularly slender crowns in a design that was based on the Roman bridge at Alcantara, Spain, built for

J.U. Raistrick's handsome Ouse Valley Viaduct near Balcombe, Sussex. *1983.*

Ribblehead Viaduct, on the Settle & Carlisle line, stands rugged and unadorned in the wild Pennine landscape. *2001.*

J.R. Broughton

the emperor Trajan in AD105. With three side arches at each end, the structure is in stone from a nearby quarry, with detailing in Aberdeen granite. Both viaducts depend on simplicity and proportion for effect. Knucklas Viaduct (1864) represents the other extreme. Standing just inside Wales from Shropshire, it was given a strong, romantic appearance by applying pseudo-medieval fortifications: crenellated parapets, prominent turrets and arrow slits, all in heavy rock-faced stone implying great strength. It must be acknowledged that for all its elaborations, it fits well into a rugged landscape in what once was turbulent border country.

When a powerful landowner realised that he could not prevent a railway from crossing his estate, he often bargained for special treatment, such as the ornamental bridge for the Earl of Lichfield in Shugborough Park in Staffordshire. The Gregorys of Stivichall Manor near Coventry succeeded in having their arms displayed on a bridge over a public road on the line to Leamington (now within the city), while a few miles further on

Lord and Lady Leigh of Stoneleigh Abbey had their respective crests put on an accommodation bridge, one on each side. If it was an attempt to keep up with the neighbours it hardly succeeded, as the bridge merely connected two fields, out of the public eye. The crenellated parapets of a bridge over the drive to Balnagown Castle near Kildary, in north-east Scotland, are decorated with the arms of the Cromarty and Sutherland families, while the gateway arch to Guthrie Castle in Angus actually carried the Arbroath & Forfar Railway over it, with the porter's lodge below. One of the most elaborate examples is Lady Wimborne's Bridge at Canford Manor (now a school) in Dorset, a rich Tudor-Gothic design by the architect Sir Charles Barry to match his remodelling of the house.

These earlier years saw the building of a number of wooden bridges. Cheap and easy to construct, they enabled a line to be opened earlier and earn revenue. Most were soon replaced by more permanent, durable structures. I.K. Brunel was the most prolific exponent. In the West Country, South Wales and the West Midlands he built the astonishing number

The graceful Montgomerie Policies Bridge, Tarbolton, Ayrshire, probably designed to enhance the Earl of Eglinton's estate. *1987*.

Lady Wimborne's Bridge, 1853, designed by Sir Charles Barry to carry the Southampton & Dorchester Railway of 1853 over the drive to Canford Manor, Dorset, where he was working on the house. *2001*.

of 441 timber bridges, 112 of them viaducts. They were tall, spindly structures, some on stone piers, others on wooden trestles of varying design, and, despite an appearance of instability, many lasted surprisingly long before being replaced by more permanent viaducts alongside. Whether the additional income earned by their rapid construction and earlier opening of the line at lower cost, compared with conventional works, outweighed the eventual cost of replacement and, probably, extra land, is problematical. Nor can it be said that, for all their daring and ingenuity, they were an adornment to the landscape, lacking the grace of brick and masonry arches.

Elsewhere some entirely different partly wooden viaducts and bridges were built in quite handsome style. They had segmental laminated timber arches on brick or stone piers, with slender radial struts or intricately patterned cross-bracing in open spandrels, imparting a degree of elegance. Their appearance can be judged from the wrought iron spans of the Ouseburn and Willington Dene viaducts at Newcastle-upon-Tyne, which in 1869 replaced the wooden arches of thirty years earlier but to near-identical design. It is a pity that the same cannot be said of Broadbottom and Dinting Vale viaducts near Glossop in north Derbyshire, built in 1845. In 1859-60 the wooden arches were replaced by unattractive wrought iron plate girders, made worse later when they had to be propped up by extra brick piers, unevenly spaced between the masonry originals, thereby destroying the symmetry. Fewer timber bridges were built in Scotland, and not many in brick. It was a country with a long tradition of stone building and fine masonry.

Where long single spans were required, the railway engineers experimented with cast iron, as had already been used by their predecessors for road and canal bridges, and aqueducts. A

favourite design was the cast iron arch with open spandrels filled with an iron trellis or struts in a variety of attractive patterns. Until it was clad in concrete in the 1960s there was a particularly handsome skewed iron arch taking the London & Birmingham Railway over the Grand Junction Canal at Kings Langley in Hertfordshire, dating from 1837. The concrete increased its lifespan but did nothing for its appearance. Belvidere Bridge of 1849, over the Severn near Shrewsbury, and the wide central arch of Waterside Viaduct near Sedbergh, Cumbria, of 1861, are two examples that make notable contributions to the landscape. Unfortunately the same can no longer be said of the three graceful central arches of the Nene Viaduct at Peterborough of 1850, which since 1924 have been dominated by trussed girders added alongside to carry extra tracks.

Some engineers were also experimenting with riveted wrought-iron, finding that it was capable of even longer spans. Four bridges from this time are acknowledged as particularly important monumental historic landmarks. First are Robert Stephenson's unique square-sectioned tubular bridges on the

The Howgill Fells form a backdrop to Waterside Viaduct, on the Ingleton–Tebay line in Cumbria. *1987.*

Watercolour by Hilary Moore

Thomas Telford's Conwy Bridge is sandwiched between the modern road bridge and Robert Stephenson's tubular railway bridge, viewed from Conwy Castle. *2011.*

J.R. Broughton

Chester & Holyhead Railway. The twin tubes of Conwy Bridge of 1848 were a prototype for his more spectacular Britannia Bridge over the Menai Strait in 1850. At Conwy, Parliament decreed that an attempt should be made to harmonise with the adjacent Conwy Castle, which the architect Francis Thompson did by adding crenellated entrance towers and turrets, although his Gothic decorative features for the tubes were omitted because of their cost. But impressive and technically important though Stephenson's tube is, it does nothing for Telford's graceful suspension bridge of 1826 alongside, obscuring it on the upstream side. The much greater height and length of the Menai Bridge, aided by Egyptian-Grecian styled stone piers, also by Thompson, gave it a natural elegance that was denied at Conwy, making it the greater tragedy when the tubes were dismantled following a disastrous fire in 1970, although the replacement steel arches, too, have their own elegance. Meanwhile, in 1849, Stephenson completed his novel cast- and wrought-iron double-deck road-and-rail High Level Bridge at Newcastle, to which we shall return in a later chapter. The fourth important landmark bridge is Brunel's equally novel Royal Albert Bridge linking Devon and Cornwall across the Tamar: two 455ft spans over 100ft high comprising huge parabolic oval wrought-iron tubes from which the rail deck is suspended by vertical iron struts braced by correspondingly curved suspension chains, an ingenious solution to height and width restrictions imposed for navigation purposes, yet making a handsome design that is the leading feature in the landscape.

By 1860 engineering and architecture were dividing into separate disciplines. Simultaneously a general decline in taste began to set in. No longer were railway structures easily assimilated into their surroundings but often were impositions upon them. In north Lancashire, Whalley Viaduct of 1850 marked an early departure from the aesthetically acceptable. A suitable clay deposit was found close by so, instead of the traditional masonry of the area, forty-nine harsh red brick arches stretch across the broad valley of the Calder, totally at odds not only with the local vernacular but with the fourth-century Cistercian abbey adjacent. Three of the arches nearest to it were given special embellishments in a crude attempt to alleviate the disharmony.

To take heavier weights and higher speeds brick structures became more ponderous. Staffordshire blue brick, widely favoured for its strength and durability, became ubiquitous. Furthermore, engineers were increasingly looking to wrought-iron girders, then steel, for bridge building, allowing much longer unsupported spans that were more easily fabricated, but destroying the concept of a bridge as a thing of beauty and distinction in the landscape. Flat trussed or latticed girders, or even uglier plate girders made up of square or rectangular sections riveted together, were so much cheaper than brickwork or masonry, and could be erected much faster. Yet for all that some large latticed girder bridges have an impressive quality that in time has become accepted in the landscape, such as the lofty Findhorn Viaduct near Tomatin (1897) and the Oykel Viaduct (1867) at Invershin on the Highland Railway in northern Scotland, the remarkable Larkhall Viaduct (1904) in Lanarkshire, no less than 174ft high, and most notably Runcorn Bridge over the Mersey, of 1869. There, the three deep 350ft-span latticed girders support the tracks along the lower members, so that in effect trains run through them instead of along the top, entering through heavily crenellated stone arches on the end piers that contribute to the powerful contrast they make with the great arch of the twentieth-century bowstring road bridge alongside. Among many less striking examples throughout Britain are two in northern Scotland: the trussed girders of Boat o'Brig Viaduct, a 1906 steel replacement of an earlier iron bridge, that does little to please; and the long latticed girders flanking a more complex hog-back trussed span that make up the 370yd long Speymouth Viaduct (1886) on the Moray coast, a fine structure in engineering terms, but in landscape terms an intrusion in the flat estuary.

Yet when latticed girders like these surmount tall spidery iron trestles, high in the air, they take on a dramatic, almost ethereal quality. Of the few that were built in Britain, only two remain. Meldon Viaduct near Okehampton, in north Devon, is 144ft high, built in 1874 on a curve which adds to the drama; Bennerley, spanning the Nottinghamshire and Derbyshire boundary (1878), is only 54ft high and more notable for its length of ¼ mile. Between Whitby and Loftus in North Yorkshire there were six in 16 miles, while the oldest and highest was Crumlin, in South Wales (1857), at 200ft, followed by two more on the Stainmore line in the northern Pennines, Deepdale, 161ft high and Belah 196ft, opened in 1861. All have been demolished. Belah was extolled by a poet as

Meldon Viaduct is one of only two iron trestles left in Britain. 144ft high, it spans the Okement Valley on northern Dartmoor. 1984.

Westmoreland's honour form'd by the skill of man
Shall ever o'er thy spacious landscape span,
And thousands wonder at the glorious sight;
Where trains shall run aloft both day and night…
Charles Davis, 1859

Although not a trestle structure, Bilston Glen Viaduct over a deep, narrow ravine, south of Edinburgh, is notable not for its prominence – its surroundings are heavily wooded – but for its remarkably complex trussed and braced wrought-iron girders, 47ft deep, forming a single span of 331ft. The longest latticed girder viaduct, indeed the longest of any kind in

The Tay Bridge is the longest in Britain, 2 miles, 50yd. *1984.*

Britain, is the Tay Bridge, nearly 2 miles, 79ft high mostly on cast-iron columns. Built in 1887, it is famous for having replaced an earlier bridge of 1879 which collapsed beneath a train in a gale, drowning seventy-nine people. That disaster heavily influenced the design of one of the most famous bridges in the world, the Forth Bridge. It employed a new principle in bridge building, cantilever construction, in a newly adopted material, steel. Completed in 1890, the height of its three great towers, 356ft., and its overall length of more than 1½ miles, invoked William Morris to call it 'the supreme specimen of all ugliness', yet today, for all its gigantic outline, angularity and enormous size, it has tremendous grace and is truly not only part of the Firth of Forth landscape but is symbolic of Scotland. In 1903 it was followed by

Over 125 years the mighty Forth Bridge has not only integrated into the landscape but has become a Scottish national monument and in 2015 was declared a World Heritage Site. *1984.*

another Scottish cantilever bridge across Loch Etive at Connel Ferry in Argyll, much smaller but built on similar triangular principles with an equally striking appearance.

The first use of concrete for bridge building appears to be on Falls of Cruachan Viaduct of 1880, overlooking Loch Awe on the line to Oban in western Scotland. Stone facings give

Glenfinnan Viaduct, on the West Highland Railway Extension, is noted as the longest of a series of viaducts that pioneered the use of mass-concrete. *1988.*

the appearance of solid masonry, but examination underneath reveals that the arches are in fact concrete, scored to look like courses. Subsequently concrete blocks were used to construct three viaducts in north Devon and north Cornwall, Derriton and Woolston (both 1898), and Calstock (1908). It was on the West Highland line extension between Fort William and Mallaig (1901) that mass concrete was first used extensively on viaducts, some faced with stone, others wholly or partly bare concrete. The best known and largest is Glenfinnan, one of the most dramatically located viaducts in Britain, 100ft high with twenty-one arches, surrounded by high mountains at the head of Loch Shiel. Because concrete does not weather as satisfactorily as stone and brick, Glenfinnan and its fellows have a certain alien character yet, perhaps because they are dwarfed by their surroundings, they have long formed an integral part of the landscape. Indeed, the whole of the 141 miles of the West Highland Railway from Craigendoran on the Clyde to Mallaig, looking across to Skye, is rightly regarded as the most scenic railway in Britain, especially north of Crianlarich. Passing through wild, mountainous country, its unobtrusive single track has few bridges and is marked only by occasional viaducts and small stations. Against such a backdrop it is also more completely absorbed into the landscape than any other railway in Britain. This same juxtaposition of a single-track railway set in a large-scale landscape, broken here and there by a viaduct, makes the Heart of Wales line from Craven Arms in Shropshire to Llandovery in Carmarthenshire almost equally unobtrusive as it slides through the hills of Central Wales. In a different way, and despite its far more numerous viaducts, England's most scenic railway, the double-track Settle & Carlisle line, is easily swallowed in the dramatic, wide open fell country of North Yorkshire.

Modern concrete bridges and viaducts will be considered in chapter 7.

Tunnels

Tunnels are rarely conspicuous landscape features; their plain, sturdy portals are usually tucked away at the end of deep cuttings. Indeed, the most visible aspects of a tunnel often are the ventilation shafts, marked by stumpy towers in the middle of fields, or artificial hillocks made from excavated spoil, indicating that there is a tunnel underneath. Some can be seen from a nearby road or may be in a public area, such as two in a park above Whitehaven Tunnel in west Cumbria, another on Clifton Down outside Bristol and, most public of all, one in a shopping precinct in the centre of Clay Cross, Derbyshire. Generally they are plain circular structures, although there are two strikingly large red brick towers close to the A5 trunk road above Kilsby Tunnel south of Rugby, 60ft in diameter and surmounted by a coronet-like circle of crenellations. The relatively few tunnel mouths that are readily visible were often given the grand treatment, built in the first phase of railway construction when there was a strong desire to impress by emphasising the magnitude of the work and, more importantly, to reassure nervous travellers about to be plunged underground. The eastern

Clay Cross tunnel shaft in the town's Market Street shopping precinct. *2001.*

portal of Box Tunnel on the London–Bristol main line of 1841 in Wiltshire comprises a strikingly classical arch that is much taller than necessary. In clear view of travellers on the busy London to Bristol main road, no doubt it was fully intended to show off the achievements of the Great Western Railway and its engineer, I.K. Brunel. The height of the arch reduces a few yards inside the tunnel, while the other end, buried away in the countryside near a very minor lane, is plain. The same criteria applies to Clayton Tunnel which takes the London & Brighton Railway, also of 1841, under the South Downs in Sussex. A bridge on the former London–Brighton road looks down on the pointed arch of the north portal, romantically decorated with turrets and castellations. Like Box, the other end is hidden away and is much plainer. Massive medieval castle gateway-like embellishments were applied with even more enthusiasm to the north portals of the tunnels at Clay Cross in Derbyshire (1840) and Bramhope in West Yorkshire (1849), but not the south ends. Curiously, in both of these instances neither end is readily accessible. Conversely, the massive Egyptian west portal to Bangor Tunnel is clearly seen from the station platform.

In the main, however, tunnel entrances were unadorned, their heavy construction and bold features being left to speak for themselves. Sometimes special styling or decoration would be applied in order to gain the support of an important landowner, such as the Egyptian east and Norman west portals of Shugborough Tunnel in Staffordshire, to satisfy the Earl of Lichfield together with the special bridge in his park. Likewise Lord Braybrooke demanded not only two unnecessary tunnels under his Essex estate at Audley End, but ornamental portals as well. For good measure one of them, Audley End Tunnel, also bears his armorial device. Neither it nor its neighbour Littlebury Tunnel, is easily seen except from a train. Both date from 1845. An extravagantly ornamental portal decorates the eastern end of Primrose Hill Tunnel, 1½ miles from Euston station, which, when it was completed, in 1837 was at the northern edge of London. The landowner, Eton College, secured a clause in the London & Birmingham Railway's Act of Incorporation stipulating that, instead of cutting through their land, the railway

The castellated
north portal of
Bramhope Tunnel.
1956.

must tunnel under it, to safeguard the amenities of future
housing development. Moreover, to prevent any possibility of
land slippage, the tunnel must have a particularly strong portal
designed to the satisfaction of the college's surveyor. The result
was monumental: a pair of huge Italianate towers flanking a
22ft high arch beneath a massive cornice, set between great
curved wing walls. The entire composition implies great
strength; at the time it was built making an imposing,
immensely dignified contribution to a landscape that, as
depicted in J.C. Bourne's 1839 lithograph, was still largely rural.
This was not for long, however, as north London suburbia
quickly spread along and over the railway, while for successive
widenings of the tracks, two additional tunnels alongside the
original, one of them a virtual replica, have reduced the effect,
later compounded by overhead electrification. The northern
portals, almost hidden away, again are quite plain.

Very occasionally a tunnel mouth was simply left as an
opening in a bare rock face, looking like a cave. Pont-y-Pant

tunnel on the Conwy Valley line in North Wales is like that, as was the west end of Brunel's Bristol No 2 Tunnel until a portal was erected in 1900.

The rural economy

The physical transformation brought about by the railways was accompanied by economic changes. The steady migration of rural workers to the growing towns, seeking better paid jobs in new industries, was speeded up. In 1851, 50 per cent of the country's population were town dwellers. By 1881 it had grown to 70 per cent. At the same time, those who stayed behind enjoyed a slow improvement in agricultural wages, especially in districts with a railway, which itself was improving agriculture. Livestock, produce, fertiliser and other farming supplies were now transported quickly and easily by rail. Droving – the movement of animals to market on the hoof – died out almost overnight. Markets themselves changed, as small ones amalgamated into larger ones located closer to, often alongside, a railway. Rural industries like wind and water-powered corn mills were replaced by large steam-powered mills sited close to railways which brought in coal and took out flour. The mill alongside the station at Shipton-under-Wychwood in Oxfordshire is an example. Lofty granaries and maltings sprang up beside railway lines, particularly in East Anglia where they were prominent features in the landscape. The milk trade was completely transformed. Hitherto small towns had relied on nearby farms; the cities on unhygienic back-yard cow keepers. Now milk could be carried in bulk, resulting in many arable farms changing to dairy, supplying a new industry that distributed fresh milk daily from large dairies and processing plants built alongside railways. Whole counties, especially west of London, made this change. Similarly horticulture changed from small market gardens to large holdings supplying fresh fruit and vegetables daily by rail to towns and to new rural canning and preserves factories.

By the 1860s new railways encouraged rural extractive industries such as quarrying, lime burning and brick and tile

making, that had been small local enterprises, to combine into larger units. Otherwise they were forced to close down. Stone for building began to be replaced by brick and slates brought in by rail. For instance, the Stonesfield quarries in Oxfordshire progressively closed during the second half of the nineteenth century, their stone roofing slabs ousted by Welsh slates.

Pont-y-Pant tunnel portal on the Conwy Valley line in North Wales is simply an opening in the rock face. *2008.* W. Fawcett

Country limekilns were abandoned as lime and cement became available by rail from large new works that formed dominant features in their local landscapes, such as those at Hope in Derbyshire, Ketton in Northamptonshire, Aberthaw in South Wales and Dunbar in East Lothian. George Stephenson was the first to open limekilns alongside a main railway when he found deposits at Ambergate during the building of the North Midland line in 1837. They grew into a large works containing twenty kilns, all now closed. Similarly with brickworks; those near a railway could expand and new ones were opened, like the series along the railway from Bletchley to Bedford and alongside the East Coast main line south of Peterborough, their tall chimneys visible from afar. The building of the railways themselves created an enormous demand for bricks. For example, the average tunnel lining took 14 million bricks per mile.

Before steam locomotives took over, the North Wales slate quarries relied on horse tramroads to convey their products to the coast for shipment by sea. Their conversion into steam-operated narrow gauge railways and consequent huge increases in production were typified not so much by the expansion of the quarries themselves as by the enormous waste tips that dominate landscapes on the western fringes of Snowdonia. In the twentieth-century rail has played a leading part in the siting of other prominent industries in the countryside, notably coal-fired power stations with tall chimneys and huge cooling towers, like those in the Trent Valley, at Drax in Yorkshire, along the Firth of Forth, and elsewhere.

The effect on villages was mixed. Much depended on the location of the station, a matter over which railway companies took great care. If one station could serve two places it would be given a double-barrelled name, such as the delightfully rural-sounding Southam & Long Itchington in Warwickshire. Having a railway station was a mark of importance. Not having one was a sign of stagnation. Many a locality near a railway but with no station petitioned a railway company to open one, sometimes several times and not always with success. An alternative was to share a station

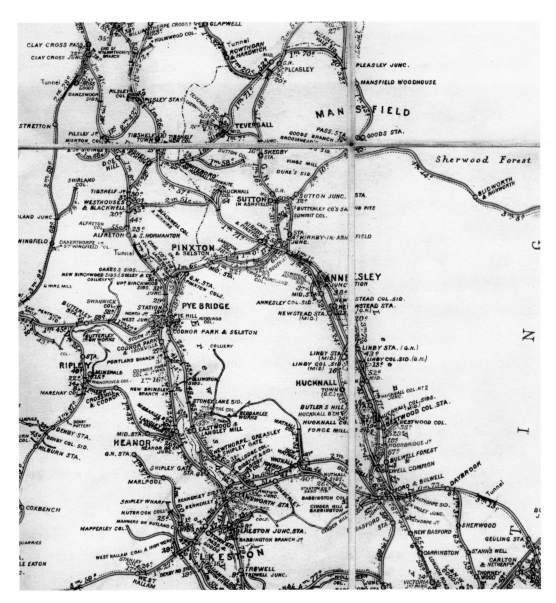

by adding a second name, as happened at Heather & Ibstock in Leicestershire, where a colliery and brickworks had grown and made Ibstock the larger place. A station often promoted village trade and expansion, the road to the station becoming lined with houses. Some villages grew to become small towns, especially if the station was at a junction where passengers changed trains, as happened at Westbury in Wiltshire, Didcot in south Oxfordshire and Carnforth, north Lancashire, where

The 1901 Railway Clearing House folding map of Derbyshire and Nottinghamshire shows the complexity of competing lines in the Erewash and Leen valleys.

small communities or enclaves of railway workers became established. Together with pure railway villages which served no other purpose than to house employees, they will be reviewed in chapter 5. On the other hand, if the railway brought the decline or closure of a local rural industry, the village population shrank as its inhabitants sought work elsewhere. Indeed, from about 1850 the general picture was one of decline as factory-manufactured goods distributed by rail began the demise of cottage crafts and industries such as glove and stocking-making, weaving, pottery and many more. In parts of Scotland families dispossessed as a result of agricultural improvements were re-housed in planned villages built for the purpose. When railways were built some were deliberately located next to a station, again to be considered in chapter 5.

Three industrial areas provide notable examples of how railways brought dramatic changes that otherwise would have been far slower. At the end of the eighteenth century the coal mining and iron smelting areas of south Staffordshire were becoming known as the Black Country, concentrated alongside a network of canals and their connecting tramroads, beyond which much of the country was still rural. Railways were a focus for development, speeding up industrialisation enormously. By the 1860s villages had grown into towns and the whole district was predominantly urban.

On each side of the boundary between Derbyshire and Nottinghamshire, two parallel valleys became heavily industrialised after they formed routes for railways. The opening of the Midland Railway up the Erewash Valley in 1847 attracted coal mining and two large ironworks, eventually requiring extensive marshalling yards in open country at Toton, followed in 1875 by the parallel line of the Great Northern. Meanwhile the Midland opened a line along the Leen Valley in 1848, steadily extended and attracting not only dense mining activity but this time two other railways, the Great Northern and the Great Central, nowhere more than ¾ mile apart, criss-crossing one another for 10 miles up the valley from complicated junctions just north of Nottingham to Sutton-in-Ashfield and

Toton marshalling
yard from the
air in 1951.

Aerofilms, courtesy
Historic England

Mansfield, together with their respective locomotive depots and,
at Annesley, a large marshalling yard.

In Scotland the rapid expansion of coal and iron production in
Ayrshire, Renfrew and northern Lanarkshire provides a similarly
vivid example of how quickly railways transformed an area that,
apart from a relatively small linen and cotton industry, was
mainly agricultural, into one that was predominantly of heavy
industry. The exploitation of extensive mineral deposits steadily
increased from the mid-1700s onward as canals and a network
of tramroads were built, but it was the steam railway that from
1826 provided the biggest stimulus. Within fourteen years there
were over 40 miles of line in Lanarkshire alone. By 1855, after
the first railway boom, there were 219 collieries and 99 iron

furnaces in the combined area, whereas in 1839 there had been only 29 furnaces in the whole of Scotland. Together, mining, iron smelting and railways had converted a large tract of the Lowlands into a centre of heavy industry. The consequence of railways was the same in the coal and iron areas of the South Wales valleys where parallel lines were particularly dense, colliery districts like south Lancashire and Durham, and other manufacturing areas of Britain such as the semi-rural textile districts in the valleys of Lancashire and Yorkshire which, by the mid-nineteenth century, had become linear urban settlements. Barry Trinder's *The Making of the Industrial Landscape* contains graphic descriptions of similar physical degradation of the rural scene in many other parts of the country.

Chapter 2

COUNTRY STATIONS AND BUILDINGS

The design of railway buildings accurately reflected all the variations, oddities and eccentricities of Victorian architectural taste. Very roughly it can be divided into three periods, although as in most broad categorisations there were many exceptions. At first the same respect for the environment that characterised early bridges and viaducts went into stations and other lineside buildings, only to become debased from around 1860, followed by a partial reassertion of good design near the end of the century.

The first phase

Most railway buildings in this early period were carefully proportioned and built from materials native to the area, fitting comfortably into the landscape. As L.F. Gregory wrote in 'Railways in the Victorian Landscape' (*Country Life*, 22 Feb, 1968), 'stations and other buildings generally had a pleasant air of comeliness.' There was an enormous variety of imaginative designs. Britain was still in the era of romanticism and the 'picturesque' that had inspired so much eighteenth-century rural building and development. Consequently many country stations reflected this spirit, echoing the gate lodges and domestic buildings that dotted the great estates. A favourite fashion was *cottage orné*, incorporating overhanging eaves, mullioned windows and tall angled chimney stacks, popularised by J.C. Loudon in his *Encyclopaedia of Cottage, Farm and Villa*

A Swiss chalet style was thought to be appropriate for Matlock Bath station in the Derbyshire Peak District. *1980.*

Architecture published in 1833. Others were deliberately built to resemble something else, such as the medieval monasticism of Battle station in Sussex, close to the Cistercian abbey, and the Swiss chalet style of Matlock Bath in Derbyshire, which was considered appropriate to the local Peak District scenery. Others were simple cottage buildings that copied the local vernacular architecture. Later on many of these early stations became outgrown and were replaced, or in our own time were closed and demolished, but enough have survived to convey the philosophy of their designers.

At this time numbers of railway companies employed good architects like John Livock of London, who designed a delightful series of Tudor and Jacobean stations on the London & Birmingham Railway's Northampton–Peterborough line of 1845, of which Wansford is the best remaining example, and the Trent Valley Railway of 1847, between Rugby and Stafford. Three station buildings survive there, and the largest and best, Atherstone, has been nicely restored. His work on these lines was notable for its unity – stations, goods sheds and crossing houses, all in matching style and built in local stone or brick.

T.M.Penson of Chester favoured half-timbering on the Shrewsbury & Chester Railway of 1846-48, again forming a complete entity, apart from two curious exceptions at Ruabon and Gobowen which were in a distinctive, delicate Florentine style. The latter still exists, again splendidly restored. Four stations between Bletchley and Bedford display the most elaborate half-timbered styling on any railway, Fenny Stratford, Woburn Sands, Ridgmont and Millbrook,situated where the line passed through the Duke of Bedford's Woburn Abbey estate. Fenny Stratford is the most picturesque. Francis Thompson designed what probably was the most delightful series of small stations anywhere, on the North Midland Railway between Derby and Leeds (1840), all different and each one notable for its delicate proportions. Only Wingfield remains, now closed and sold. Thompson did the opposite

In 1846-48 T.M. Penson favoured a carefully executed Florentine style for Gobowen station, Shropshire. *1994.*

Wadhurst station, Kent, typifies William Tress's Italian villa style on the Tunbridge Wells–Hastings line in Kent. *1958.*

on the Chester & Holyhead Railway (1848), where he devised a common plan but with variations, so that no two were identical. Holywell is the most elaborate. Another London architect, William Tress, who designed Battle, executed a number of other stations for the South Eastern Railway, particularly a series between Tunbridge Wells and Hastings, some resembling Italian villas, others small Tudor manor houses. George Townsend Andrews of York was one of the most prolific railway architects in this period, producing high quality work throughout north-east England. Like Tress, he was equally proficient in devising classical and Tudor designs, as well as a plain, functional station building that was simultaneously economical and distinctive. Beyond the Tyne the Newcastle architect Benjamin Green designed for the Newcastle & Berwick Railway (1847) one of the finest series of stations in the Tudor-Jacobean style in Britain, each one different and accompanied by a matching stone goods shed. Fortunately most of them have survived, in or out of railway ownership.

Only one railway architect in this period was in the top rank of his profession, Sir William Tite, a shrewd and wealthy London practitioner who combined his architectural work with railway directorships and many other business interests. While he is best known for rebuilding the Royal Exchange in the City of London, his prolific railway output included all the stations on the London & Southampton Railway of 1840 and many on its successor the London & South Western; the Lancaster & Carlisle, Caledonian and Scottish Central railways (1846-48) which formed a near continuous line from Lancaster to Perth; and three lines in northern France. He developed a distinctive style for some of his LSWR stations, but was equally at home with classical or Tudor-Gothic, and he had great regard for local materials, while his small stations in north-west England and Scotland were well in keeping with their surroundings.

Most engineers at this time were content to leave station design to architects, except I.K. Brunel on the Great Western Railway, who took on the task himself, very successfully so far as country stations were concerned. He evolved a simple design: a small single-storey

Tress abruptly interrupted the series on the same line at Frant and Etchingham, the latter seen here. *1983*.

Acklington station, Northumberland, by Newcastle architect Benjamin Green, opened in 1847. *1966.*

Tudor-styled building with a steep roof and an all-round awning. Unfortunately, Culham, between Didcot and Oxford (1844), is the only survivor that is complete and still in use. A later variant was Italianate, with a hipped roof extending out on all four sides to form an integral awning. Both types were built in several sizes in stone, brick or flint according to locality, appearing in the West Country, the West Midlands and South Wales from the late 1840s into the 1860s. Mortimer in Berkshire and Chepstow in Monmouthshire are two Italianate examples, while Charlbury in Oxfordshire is a well-preserved wooden type. Brunel also designed a small, very plain but functional station building, with a gabled roof, a flat awning at front and rear, and perhaps a bay window on one end. Some of these also were wooden. St Germans in Cornwall (1859) is a survivor of this type. The very uniformity of these stations precludes any pretence that they acknowledged local vernacular building, yet their neat compactness and use of local materials somehow fitted them into their localities.

Accompanying the work of accomplished architects there were countless modest cottage-like stations, often by unknown designers, completely at home in their settings, like Uffington & Barnack in Cambridgeshire – possibly by Sancton Wood –

and Thorpe-on-the-Hill in Lincolnshire, both dating from 1846. Some were by local craftsmen, such as the oldest building at a present-day working railway station, the small cottage building on the pioneer Stockton & Darlington Railway at Heighington of c1827, which appears to be the work of the superintendent of masonry, John Carter. Scottish country stations in the early period also tended to be small cottage types, predominantly in stone as would be expected, plain but seemly, with few of the architectural flourishes of some of their English counterparts. The original Monifieth station building on the Dundee & Arbroath Railway of 1838 is low and T-shaped, its only adornment a single spike on top of a gable. Deep overhanging gables were typical of many small stations; Drem (1846) east of Edinburgh, Errol (1847) in Perthshire, and Cummertrees and Kirkconnel (1850) in Dumfriesshire are examples.

Not all station buildings were of such good quality. Many were wooden, built for economy, although some survived surprisingly long. The South Eastern Railway was particularly partial to them and some are still in use between Redhill and Ashford (1842) and on other parts of the system. They were to a design that evolved in batches for over fifty years and, despite their cheapness it can be said that environmentally they were in the Kentish clapboard tradition. For much the same reason the Eastern Counties Railway built several extraordinary two-storey wooden stations that were quite untraditional, their exposed timber framing imparting a distinctly North American or colonial flavour, or possibly copying Dutch houses inspired by the historical links between East Anglia and the Low Countries. Manea, Stonea and Black Bank between Ely and March (1847-51), and Fakenham in Norfolk (1849), were examples, now demolished, although several wooden crossing houses remain on the system.

W.W. Tomlinson in his classic *The North Eastern Railway: its Rise and Development* (1914) remarked that, apart from Andrews' and Green's work, 'the stations on some early lines were built with a greater regard for economy than convenience,' a comment that applied countrywide. More than a few were quite wretched, like Sough station, between Bolton and Blackburn, of 1847, which a photograph taken about 1860 shows as a dilapidated wooden

shack with a ragged tarpaulin roof. Fortunately it was out of view in a cutting, and was reputed to have fallen down when caught on a passenger's coat button.

As with ornamental bridges, an influential landowner could acquire a special station as a condition of support for a new railway. Two in north Staffordshire had Italian villa-type buildings: Alton Towers (1849) for the Earl of Shrewsbury and Trentham (1848) for the Duke of Sutherland, both possibly by Sir Charles Barry. Not far away a third, Sandon (1849), reflected the Jacobean gate lodges in the Earl of Harrowby's Sandon Park nearby. All became public stations. Hall Dene (1855), however, was built by the Marquis of Londonderry for his sole use on his own line, the Londonderry Railway in County Durham. It was a curious building in red and white banded brick.

The middle period, c1865-85
This was a time when much smaller-scale Victorian architecture became insensitive and unimaginative, in the case of railways changing the fragile balance between them and the scenery, a

balance which L.F. Gregory described as lying 'between sensibility and philistinism'. The steady advance of brick and slated buildings into areas where hitherto they had been unknown began to accelerate, reflected in railway buildings where now the prime consideration was economy. The average railway company dividend in 1850-75 was only 3.65 per cent, and some companies, notably the Great Eastern and the London Chatham & Dover, in the mid-1860s, were in receivership. On the other hand, several large companies like the London & North Western and the North Eastern were consistently paying 6.8 to 9 per cent. But whatever their circumstances, the railways practiced strict economy, whether to reduce debt or to maintain dividends. Diversity in building work increasingly gave way to standardisation, regardless of location. Each company developed its own distinctive style, changing it from time to time. For example, from around 1870 the Great Western erected throughout its system numerous single-storey buildings to a common design and built in a particularly harsh red brick obtained from either Ruabon, on the border of North Wales, or Cattisbrooke Brickworks at Bristol. The London & North Western greatly favoured distinctive timber

At the end of the nineteenth century, the Great Western Railway descended to a standard ugly red-brick style regardless of location. This example is at Wilmcote, near Stratford-upon-Avon, built in 1906. *1981.*

A typical standard London & North Western Railway wooden station of the late 1800s at Clifton Mill, near Rugby, photographed in 1952 and closed a year later.

buildings, prefabricated at its Crewe Works, including sectional huts that could be erected singly or in series according to requirements, whether as platform buildings, goods yard cabins or, on occasions, small signal boxes. The Great Eastern and Great Northern companies were partial to undistinguished two-storey station buildings in pale yellow or buff brick; the Lancashire & Yorkshire a mixture of rather drab single-storey buildings in stone or yellow brick. In 1887 the London & South Western earned from *The Builder* some characteristic acid criticism of stations it had enlarged and rebuilt between Barnes and Mortlake, an area becoming popular with commuters although still quite rural. 'These were fairly pretty country stations…all quietly and nicely designed [by William Tite]. They have now been "translated" and are the ugliest stations near the Metropolis….Mortlake being an especially abominable "contraption" of iron, wood and zinc. We ought to improve in railway architecture as we have in other branches of the art.'

There were exceptions to the mediocrity. The Midland Railway was early in introducing a measure of standardisation on its Leicester–Hitchin line, opened in 1857, where it built a series of stations that varied in size, comprising a two-storey gabled house attached to a single-storey office building. Despite their uniformity they had the great merit of using different local building materials as the line proceeded southward: red brick in the clay country, then white, followed by golden ironstone, pale grey limestone and then red brick again. The Midland also was notable for a 'twin pavilion' type of building, essentially comprising a single-storey pitched-roofed building parallel to the platform flanked by a pair of gabled projections or pavilions, forming a central recess that was wholly or partially enclosed as a waiting area. Larger stations might have three pavilions, and from the 1870s the type appeared all over the company's widespread system from Gloucestershire to Cumbria. A variety of decoration was applied, such as intricately shaped bargeboards and lozenge-patterned iron window frames. On the Settle & Carlisle line they came in three sizes, while local stone, changing as the line went northward, maintained a commendable measure of harmony with the landscape. Long Marton and Appleby were exceptions in red brick, the latter inexplicably in a town where red sandstone buildings predominated. The Great Northern and several other railways also built some stations in this

Langwathby on the Settle & Carlisle line, 1876, represents a typical Midland Railway 'twin pavilion' style station of the period in its most elaborate form. *2002.* J.R. Broughton

style, the GNR's rather bleak and lacking the Midland's stylishness. Those of the Manchester, Sheffield & Lincolnshire and the Cheshire Lines, too, were in better taste and more ornate, not unlike the Midland's. The North Eastern's own variation had a two-storey central building, sometimes with one of the pavilions two-storeyed as well, and often in local stone.

The twin pavilion type took root in Scotland somewhat earlier than in England. East Linton, on the East Coast main line of the North British south of Edinburgh, for instance, dates from 1864. Also in the 1860s the Highland Railway had some delightful cottage-type stations north of Inverness, perfectly plain as befitted the bare landscape and built from large rugged stone blocks that blended perfectly. Ardgay and Fearn (1864) are examples, while Rogart (1868) is an enlarged version of a typical crofter's cottage.

The end of the century

The last two decades of the nineteenth century and the first of the twentieth saw something of a return to the stylistic ethics of the early years, in what became known as the Domestic Revival and the Arts and Crafts movement. It was a reaction against mass-produced, standardised fashions in building. The London & South Western Railway redeemed itself by building a series of charming stations on the Meon Valley line in Hampshire in 1903. Easily absorbed into the landscape, they truly reflected Arts and Crafts ideas and were some of the best latter-day country stations. Although the South Eastern continued to build in wood, somewhat uncharacteristically it also erected a few quite commendable stations like Sandling and Nutfield in a homely rustic style, both in 1888. The neighbouring London, Brighton & South Coast Railway's endeavours in the Arts and Crafts movement earned

Sandling station, Kent, opened by the South Eastern Railway in 1888, was one of the few built in the Domestic Revival style then starting to become popular. *1955.*

praise from *The Builder*; two-storeyed station buildings, some tile-hung like Lavant (1881), and some like Horsted Keynes (1882) with decorated plasterwork in pseudo half-timbering, accompanied by spacious platform awnings and generous accommodation. But in truth they were too large and tall to be said to sit comfortably in their surroundings. Most of the other railways confined new rural work in this period mainly to a continuation of standard styles or, in the case of the Great Central's new line opened in 1899 down the centre of England from Nottinghamshire to London, a new style that was particularly uninspired. With two exceptions, all twenty-two intermediate

Lavant represented the London, Brighton & South Coast Railway's somewhat dominant response to Domestic Revival styling, opened in 1881 and in a rather sorry state when photographed long after it closed in 1935, although it seems to have been used occasionally for Goodwood race traffic afterwards. *1968.*

stations were virtually identical in red brick with blue dressings, completely regardless of locality. These years also saw the introduction of reinforced concrete, largely pioneered by William Marriott, engineer of the Midland & Great Northern Joint Railway, which ran across south Lincolnshire and Norfolk to Cromer, Lowestoft and Norwich. He used it for fence and signal posts, platform walls, nameboards and a variety of other purposes, including a few houses and station buildings. Rather surprisingly, the earliest appears to have been the Highland Railway's concrete station building of 1871 at Helmsdale, on the Far North line beyond Inverness.

The Scottish equivalent of the Domestic Revival produced some good, unpretentious country stations, many distinguished by hipped roofs with slightly-curved lower ends, known in Scotland as bell-cast roofs. There was a notable, near-identical series on the West Highland line of 1894 and its extension of 1901, a total of 141 miles from the Clyde to Mallaig. They were in an attractive Swiss chalet style deemed appropriate to the mountainous area, roofed and partly clad with imported Swiss wooden shingles. The Caledonian Railway also built several attractive Domestic Revival stations; Fort Matilda (1889) was a

Quorn & Woodhouse in the standard pattern of stations on the Great Central Railway's new line to London, opened in 1899, closed in 1963, but reopened by the heritage Great Central Railway. *2001.*

good example. During this period the Highland Railway built several twin-pavilion type stations with strong Scottish characteristics. At Moy (1897) and Pitlochry (1890) the stone main buildings of this type were accompanied by substantial wooden bellcast-roofed buildings on the opposite platforms.

The period also saw the introduction of standard designs for goods sheds, weighbridge houses and other buildings. Some of the earlier ones were quite pretty, matching the passenger buildings, while others were plain wooden sheds. On the Great Western, Brunel's early goods sheds often were built from black tarred planks, jarring with his neat stations and rather out of character for him. As increasing traffic outgrew earlier buildings they were replaced by standard types. The London & North Western, for instance, put up a great many distinctive red brick goods sheds at country stations throughout its system.

Stations on the West Highland Railway were built in a Swiss chalet style thought in 1894 to be appropriate for western Scotland. Here is Upper Tyndrum when it was named Tyndrum Upper. *1988.*

Houses

From their earliest days railway companies provided houses for some of their employees, especially in country districts where accommodation was hard to find. In this they followed the example of the canals, which built lock-keepers' cottages, and the turnpike

trusts' toll-houses. They were mainly for crossing-keepers, workers on the line and, later, signalmen working at isolated boxes. Station staff housing often was incorporated into station buildings or grouped with them. Like stations, the first houses were in the picturesque tradition, fitting easily into the landscape, but in time, as with everything else, standardised styles prevailed regardless, although it has to be

The red-brick goods shed at Castle Ashby, Northamptonshire, is typical of London & North Western Railway late nineteenth century practice. *1968.*

acknowledged that the overall degree of accommodation in railway houses was a vast improvement on the average workers' dwellings of the day. Some Midland, North Eastern and Scottish railways' houses looked rather better than those of many other companies by the use of local stone, while as late as 1880 the Callander & Oban Railway built some very seemly single-storey lineside cottages. But generally the later railway houses tended to look the same throughout their respective lines, none more so than those of the London & North Western which had well over 4,000 houses. Gaunt looking, in pale-red brick with bright red dressings, they appeared all over that extensive system from London to Carlisle, Swansea to Leeds, quite regardless of locality, whether urban or rural. Apart from roofing slates, everything, including the bricks, came from the company's works at Crewe. Many still stand today, singly or in terraces, uncompromisingly prominent in the landscape.

Signal boxes, engine sheds and yards
The concentration of signalling control in one place, a signal box, was a gradual process dating mainly from the 1860s, in which many railway companies employed specialist signalling contractors, each having its own design. With very few exceptions the basis was a two-storey structure, with the

The gatekeeper's house at Hilton Crossing, North Staffordshire Railway. *1984.*

A more elaborate house at Wollascott Crossing, between Shrewsbury and Chester. *1994.*

Blackford signal box, between Stirling and Perth, represents a typical Caledonian Railway type. *1990.*

operating floor above, giving the signalman a good view of the line, and the interlocking mechanism below, a building type that continued until mechanical signalling became outmoded in our own day. After about 1880 the companies increasingly set up their own signalling departments, each producing its own distinctive standard style of box that changed from time to time, producing some very attractive designs by which each railway could be readily identified. Mainly they were wooden above and brick below, although a considerable number were all-brick or all-wood. The North British Railway in particular had a standard all-brick box that was particularly neat. Together with semaphore signals they were very familiar and distinctive in the railway scene but, away from large junctions, boxes in open country seldom created significant intrusion because they were small. Occasionally a signal box might be specially designed to match a station. Nutfield in Sussex, for instance, an Arts and Crafts station we have already noted, had a delightfully matching signal box; all those on the West Highland line formed an entity with the stations; while the box at Tenbury Wells in Worcestershire was in matching stone attached to the station building. To give the signalman a good view some boxes were very tall. Kittybrewster South signal box on the Great North of Scotland Railway near Aberdeen, for example, was a lofty structure that enabled the signalman to see over an adjoining bridge. Although the wooden superstructure was the company's standard product – not unattractive – the tall base was in fine ashlar granite that fully respected local building tradition. This is more than could be said of the equally tall box at Northenden on the Cheshire Lines south of Manchester. The London & North Western in particular often favoured tall red brick bases for its standard box introduced in the mid-1870s, a somewhat austere design found throughout its extensive system regardless of location.

Most country junctions and many branch line termini had an engine shed, and like stations they were in all shapes and sizes.

Wareham signal box, Dorset, is one of several London & South Western Railway designs. *1988.*

The lofty Cheshire Lines signal box at Northenden Junction, near Stockport, is a local landmark. *1984.*

A branch line
engine shed:
Moretonhampstead,
Devon, restored
and now used for
other purposes.
2009. M.R. Hart.

Some of the small ones for one or two locomotives were not unattractive in stone or brick, until inevitably they became contaminated by smoke and dirt. Others were more utilitarian, in wood or corrugated iron. Oxenholme, a country junction on the West Coast main line in south Cumbria, had a shed for twelve locomotives, a standard red brick building that was quite out of tune with its location. Twelve miles further north another country junction, Tebay, was in a dramatic setting in the eastern Lakeland hills. Two companies' lines met there, each having its own shed, adding very visible atmospheric pollution to even greater physical intrusion. Such duplication was not uncommon at other locations where two railways met; Midhurst in Sussex and Keith in north-east Scotland were examples, although fortunately the sheds were quite small. Larger ones might also have an elevated water tank, a boiler house and chimney, coaling plant and perhaps a small gas works for lighting. More than a few larger sheds intruded in rural locations, such as Templecombe in Somerset which kept as many as ten locomotives. Some were on particularly sensitive sites, like Penzance, on the Cornish coast a mile or so from the station and literally at the head of the beach. The sheds at Llandudno Junction on the Conwy estuary opposite the castle, and Hellifield, on the edge of the Yorkshire Dales, were in similarly prominent locations, the latter another junction between two companies where each had its own yard and shed.

Marshalling yards and sorting sidings needed large areas of flat land. Usually they were on the edge of towns and industrial conurbations, like Feltham in Middlesex, in time becoming assimilated into them as we shall see later. Some were in open country, however, such as Whitemoor, outside March in Cambridgeshire; Woodford, a Northamptonshire junction; Rowsley in the Derbyshire Peak District; Cadder Yard north east of Glasgow; and Severn Tunnel Junction in South Wales, each accompanied by an engine shed. Not only was there visual intrusion and smoke, but the noise of shunting too.

Chapter 3

THE COAST

R ailways intruded on the coastline in two ways: they ran along it, changing its appearance, and they ran to it, giving access to resorts and ports, making them grow. In some cases they created new ones.

Railways along the coast
Railway engineers chose coastal routes because they were shorter or easier than inland, sometimes both. Brunel considered an inland route for the South Devon Railway between Exeter and Newton Abbot but discarded it in favour of a longer coastal line that avoided heavy gradients and tunnelling, although he still had the expense of building sea walls and four short tunnels

The Great Western line along the South Devon coast is probably the best-known and most scenic of Britain's coastal railways. It begins here at Starcross. *1981.*

J.R. Broughton

along the foot of the cliffs for 4½ miles between Dawlish Warren and Teignmouth, the best known and most spectacular of Britain's coastal railways. Conversely, William Cubitt chose a course for the South Eastern Railway between Folkestone and Dover along the foot of the famous white cliffs because not only was it the shortest but because an inland route was impracticable without a major detour. Even then the 4 miles required almost 2 miles of tunnel and the entire removal of Round Down Cliff by blasting. The overlying chalk was so loose that he needed to bore twin single-line tunnels through Shakespeare Cliff, tall and narrow with a lancet-arch profile. At the Dover end originally the line was carried along the foreshore on a wooden trestle. Along Cardigan Bay the Cambrian Railways had a cliff-foot line north and south of Barmouth, the latter section much the longer and particularly prone to rock falls, to the extent that eventually an avalanche shelter was built at Friog Rocks. The big disadvantage of shoreline routes is the risk of damage during storms, vividly demonstrated many times, most recently in the winter of 2014 when sections of track at Dawlish and Teignmouth in South Devon, on the coast of north-west Cumbria, and elsewhere, were washed out.

Wherever possible coastal railways took advantage of raised beaches; linear platforms along a shoreline caused by wave action during a long period. In some places they may be a short distance inland following the creation over time of intervening sand dunes, and often grown over. The longest sections are on the Highland Railway north of Inverness along Beauly, Cromarty and Dornoch Firths before the line loops inland through Lairg to avoid difficult country as far as the Mound, thence taking to the coast again northward for almost 20 miles to Helmsdale, including the former Dornoch branch. The only other break is at Golspie where the railway goes round the back of Dunrobin Castle, seat of the dukes of Sutherland. As the line here was built at the expense of the third duke he was entitled to divert it to prevent it from spoiling his view. The courses of the lines from Kilwinning to Largs and Troon in south-west Scotland also are largely dictated by raised beaches. Estuaries provided easy routes for railways. The Camel estuary between Wadebridge and Padstow in north Cornwall, both

sides of the Exe in south Devon, and 11 miles up the Tywi estuary in South Wales are examples, requiring the straightening of shore lines and the building of embankments. Bridges were needed to cross side creeks and inflowing rivers, often substantial ones such as the Tamerton and Tavy viaducts on the Tamar estuary in Devon. Estuaries could also form a barrier that had to be crossed by an embankment and a bridge or viaduct, as was done across the Mawddach and Loughor estuaries in Wales. In all these cases the ecology and tidal patterns were changed by the railway, creating different flows, sandbanks and shorelines, sometimes providing opportunities for land reclamation. The remarkable Montrose Basin underwent considerable changes after the Arbroath & Montrose Railway bridged the River Esk at its mouth. In places the railway took advantage of earlier embankments built for land drainage, or traversed reclaimed land. The Great Western and Llanelly railways crossed land behind the Bewick Embankment close to Llanelli, in return being obliged to contribute to its

The viaduct over the Leven estuary near Ulverston has the Lake District mountains as a backdrop. *2013.*

The wooden Barmouth Viaduct over the Mawddach estuary, photographed before 1898.

maintenance, while in North Wales the narrow gauge Festiniog Railway used the Traeth Mawr Embankment to cross the mouth of the Glaslyn estuary at Porthmadog. Two other narrow gauge lines and the Cambrian Railways traversed the reclaimed land beyond it, the Cambrian continuing to another embankment across the Dwyryd estuary at Penrhyndeudraeth, adding a toll road alongside. In Sutherland, the Highland Railway's Dornoch branch used The Mound, a land reclamation embankment built by Thomas Telford in 1817. In Norfolk land reclamation schemes along the River Yare were aided by the building of the Yarmouth & Norwich Railway in 1844.

The embankment carrying the final 2 miles of the Preston & Wyre Railway to Fleetwood was less successful. It was constructed in 1840 to reclaim an area of tidal marsh and sand alongside the Wyre estuary, on which a new port and town were planned by a large landowner, Sir Peter Hesketh Fleetwood, and named after himself. But because of financial difficulties the town and docks were built at the seaward end beyond the marsh, leaving the embankment solely to carry the railway, which it did for eleven years until it became unstable and was abandoned in favour of a new line on the landward side.

Railways projected along or close to cliff tops often presented fewer difficulties. Best known are the Scottish sections of the East Coast main line between Berwick-on-Tweed and Burnmouth, and Cockburnspath and Torness, affording spectacular views seawards. North of the Forth Bridge, after low coastal sections in Fife and Angus, it moves inland, rejoining the coast at Dundee as far as Montrose, where again it goes inland, before returning to the coast beyond Stonehaven to rise up as a cliff-top railway to Aberdeen. In north Norfolk, the railway from Mundesley to Cromer kept to the high ground, never more than ¾ mile from the cliffs. On the North Yorkshire coast, the line from Scarborough to Whitby and Saltburn

The East Coast main line along the coast near Lamberton, north of Berwick. *2015.* W. Fawcett

The railway and station at Colwyn Bay separate the town from the promenade. *1962.*

Aerofilms, courtesy Historic England

essentially was a cliff-top route, less easy as it had to avoid deep valleys by making inland loops or, as at Robin Hood's Bay, Sandsend and Staithes, crossing them close to the sea on tall viaducts. They have now been demolished except for Larpool Viaduct, a short way inland from Whitby.

Two coastal railways combine the features we have considered, materially changing the coastal landscape. The Chester & Holyhead Railway of 1848 runs along the edge of the North Wales coast nearly all the way from Flint to Colwyn Bay, deviating slightly inland between Talacre and Rhyl, much of it on a low embankment on a raised beach along the shoreline, enabling large tracts of land to be reclaimed. After passing inland to Conwy it regains the coast as a cliff-foot line, tunnelling through headlands at Penmaenbach and Penmaenmawr to Llanfairfechan where it again curves inland towards Bangor. The second line is much the longest of its kind: 52 miles along the Cumbrian coast from Arnside to Maryport, excluding a break where it crosses the Furness peninsula between Ulverston and Barrow and a short inland deviation at Whitehaven. The line was built in sections by several companies between 1847 and 1857. On leaving the ¼ mile-long low viaduct over the Kent estuary at Arnside it traverses nearly 7 miles of embankment alongside Morecambe Bay to a similar viaduct nearly ½ mile long across the estuary of the River Leven at Ulverston. Because they are low girder structures they do not

Preserved locomotive *Flying Scotsman* takes the *Cumbrian Coast Express* charter train along the edge of Morecambe Bay near Grange-over-Sands. *1987.*

J.R. Broughton

over-intrude in the flat landscape, but the embankments altered the local topography, giving renewed impetus to earlier drainage schemes that resulted in the reclamation of some 20,000 acres of salt marsh, while the viaducts affected tidal flows, radically changing the configuration of the estuaries more than any previous human activity. North of Barrow-in-Furness the line winds around the Duddon estuary, crossing it at its narrowest point before taking advantage of the coast northward for 23 miles, first on the coastal plain, including sections on the shoreline, and then along the base of cliffs before going inland behind St Bees Head. After tunnelling under the back of Whitehaven, the railway regains the shore and takes another spectacular cliff-base route to Workington before finally following a raised beach to Maryport.

Coastal resorts

Very few seaside resorts did not owe their popularity and growth to railways, which in some cases were their origins. In doing so, railways changed the coast to a greater degree than many rural landscapes, as a few representative examples will show.

Brighton had long been a fashionable resort when the London & Brighton Railway was opened in 1841, introducing mass travel. Royal and aristocratic patronage quickly departed in the face of advancing middle-class holidaymakers and day excursionists. The town was transformed from a place of some 7,000 inhabitants in 1846 to 47,000 in 1881. In 1852 the railway company established its works there, introducing a measure of industrialisation to Brighton. Blackpool started later. From a modest 2,000 people in 1841, four years before the railway arrived, its population only doubled over the next twenty years until, after a second line was opened in 1863, the town grew enormously, reaching 50,000 by the century's end. In addition to its popularity as a holiday resort, Blackpool attracted huge numbers of day trippers, estimated in 1900 to be three million a year, to the extent that in 1903 a third, more direct line was opened. With adjoining Lytham and St Annes it also became a residential dormitory for the better-off inhabitants of

The coastal railway at Parton in west Cumbria is equally dramatic. *1989.*

J.R. Broughton

Blackpool North Station is a prominent feature in that part of the town, capable of handling large crowds. *1966.*

Manchester and the Lancashire cotton towns, attracted to living there by fast, frequent train services. By 1931 the population was over 100,000.

In a similar way Southport became a commuter town for Liverpool, as well as a resort. In 1831 it held 3,000 people, but following the opening of a railway from the city in 1851, and then lines from Manchester, it grew to house over 18,000 thirty years later. In 1931, by which time it was served by electric trains from Liverpool, the population was 78,000. The railway played a similar role at Southend. In the early 1800s it was a quiet resort popular with Londoners and most easily reached by river. The opening of a railway in 1856 prompted the big railway contractor Thomas Brassey to invest in building development. In 1871 the population was just over 5,000, but after a new, more direct line in 1881 brought London within fifty minutes travelling time, it grew to nearly 71,000 by 1911. A line entering from the north contributed to the expansion, and today's Southend conurbation extends eastwards along 7½ miles of the Thames estuary from Leigh-on-Sea to Shoeburyness.

Several resorts resisted a railway, fearful that it would injure their reputations as select watering places. Until 1862 visitors to Bournemouth relied on a horse-bus service from Poole Station, 6 miles away. In that year the railway came to Christchurch, 4 miles away, but it was not until 1870 and 1874 that two lines were opened on roundabout routes to Bournemouth itself, terminating on opposite sides of the town, with which a majority of the inhabitants seemed content. However, a vocal minority pressed for a more direct line from Christchurch which was opened in 1885, together with a cross-town connection and a new central station. The town then grew rapidly from 28,000 in

For the same reason Southend-on-Sea Central Station also is prominent in the local townscape. *2001.*

1891 to over 78,500 in 1911. Bournemouth was now near enough to centres of population to attract excursion traffic, despite which it retained a degree of exclusivity.

Bournemouth's chief rival, Torquay, sought to be even more select and largely remained so. A smaller resort enjoying an even milder climate, it developed both before and after the South Devon Railway arrived in 1848. Located on a branch line beyond the reach of most day excursions, it grew to only half Bournemouth's size while eventually enjoying a service of through trains from London, the Midlands and the north that furthered its popularity with the middle classes. Torquay's desire to remain exclusive was helped by Paignton, the next station 2 miles down the line, which deliberately set out to attract working-class patronage. Both towns remained separate municipalities until local government reorganisation in 1974.

Because Weston-super-Mare feared it would lose its select clientele when the Bristol & Exeter Railway was promoted, the main line passed it by and for ten years the town had to be content with a horse-drawn coach on a 1½ mile branch. Steam trains began in 1851, by which time Weston was regretting its decision. Even so, despite the handicap of the branch line, the railway brought expansion and excursions began running from

Saltburn Station serves a cliff-top resort. *1990.*

Bristol and further afield. In 1884 the branch was replaced by a loop line, and with a new enlarged station the resort's expansion accelerated.

Railway-inspired development transformed two sections of coastline more than any other. On the Thanet coast of Kent, branches of the South Eastern Railway served Whitstable, Margate and Ramsgate. Although they were popular with Londoners, there was no direct line and steamers successfully competed with the railway. As other resorts were brought within easy reach of the capital by rail, trade fell off until in 1863 a new railway, the London Chatham & Dover, opened a line along the coast. It also served Herne Bay, Birchington-on-Sea, Westgate-on-Sea and Broadstairs, providing a direct service from London that soon attracted commuters as well as holidaymakers. In the 1920s the Southern Railway rationalised the lines in Thanet and closed the former South Eastern branches. Meanwhile Margate had outstripped Ramsgate and a few years later all but six of the 16 miles along the coast from Whitstable had become built up.

The other is the North Wales coast where, as we have already seen, the Chester & Holyhead Railway ran close to the sea, allowing land to be reclaimed. At the same time, between Prestatyn and Colwyn Bay, and Penmaenmawr and Llanfairfechan, it provided the impetus for entirely new holiday resorts, stretching for some 17 miles in all. When the line opened in 1848 there were only three stations on the combined length; a year later three more were added, and five more by the end of the century, eleven in total, all catering for holiday traffic. Before the railway was built none were places of any real consequence. Rhyl and Abergele were the largest, enjoying a modest patronage, and immediately after the railway came they began to expand, Abergele slowly and Rhyl much faster, from some 3,000 inhabitants to 13,500 by 1931. Abergele's population by that time had actually fallen. Its centre was nearly a mile from the station on the shore whereas, although the station at Rhyl was nearly ½ mile inland, the town's core became centred around it. Colwyn Bay developed from nothing. It grew alongside the slightly inland village of Colwyn – later renamed Old Colwyn –

and until 1862 it had no station. Then one was built next to the shore and soon the town became the largest resort on the coast, its population reaching 20,800 in 1931. The fact that the railway ran along the head of the beach, cutting off the new promenade from the town, did nothing to hinder growth. The Chester & Holyhead played a prominent part in these developments by various means, such as issuing cut-price tickets for new house-owners at Abergele. The company's chairman, the prominent railway contractor Samuel Morton Peto, bought land there and laid out houses, building on his earlier success as a railway contractor-cum-director in transforming Lowestoft from a small, decaying port into a thriving resort. In North Wales, improved train speeds and frequency brought Manchester and Liverpool within daily commuting distance for businessmen, adding to urban growth along the coast. By the end of the century the company's successor, the London & North Western Railway, was obliged to widen most of the line to four tracks in order to handle the holiday traffic.

North Wales' second largest resort, Llandudno, developed quite differently, pre-dating the railway. Under the strict control of the landowner, Lord Mostyn, it was deliberately created as a select resort with wide streets and gracious buildings on a carefully planned promenade curving around the bay. Development was restrained, so that when the Chester & Holyhead built a branch to Llandudno in 1858 the population was only some 1,300. Under the influence of the railway it grew to 5,000 by 1885 and, when it attracted a share of the commuter traffic, to 13,500 by 1931.

The Duke of Devonshire exercised similar control over the development of Eastbourne in Sussex, again to ensure that it was suitably select after the railway opened in 1849. But at Skegness, Lord Scarbrough had fewer qualms when the railway arrived in 1873, quickly laying out a town, followed by other developers. The unscrupulous railway magnate George Hudson, the 'Railway King', attempted to develop the small port of Whitby after gaining control of the Whitby & Pickering Railway, but failed, although later, after rail connections to the town had been extended, its growth as a resort revived. In 1863 the inhabitants of Ilfracombe, a small port in north Devon that was becoming fashionable, wanted a railway. For eleven years their plans were frustrated by a powerful landowner until, in 1874, a branch from Barnstaple was finally achieved, albeit on fierce gradients to an inconvenient station at the top of a hill above the town.

When another successful contractor, Thomas Savin, tried to emulate the North Wales coast's popularity further south on Cardigan Bay in the early 1860s, he and the Cambrian Railways failed, bankrupting themselves. The nearest centres of population, the Midlands, were too far away along a winding single-track railway through the mountains of mid-Wales. Aberystwyth developed, and to a lesser extent Barmouth, but other places along the coast such as Tywyn and Harlech remained small, popular with those seeking a quiet holiday in attractive scenery.

Resorts on the Ayrshire coast developed from small ports like Ardrossan, Troon and Ayr itself. The opening of lines along the coast attracted holiday traffic, and then commuters from Glasgow. Largs, for example, grew from a population of 700 in

Wemyss Bay Station is alongside the Clyde steamer pier. *1995.*

1811 to 3,200 in 1891, Ayr from 8,000 to 24,000 and Troon from a mere 200 to 3,300. The last was by far the most popular with Glasgow business folk, reaching 8,500 inhabitants in 1931, almost entirely attributable to the railway.

A multitude of smaller resorts around Britain owed their development to later extensions of the railway network, such as Mablethorpe and Sutton-on-Sea on a loop line along the Lincolnshire coast, although at the latter a railway-inspired port came to nothing. Small ports and fishing villages enjoyed modest development when they found themselves at the end of a branch line; for example Clacton and Frinton in Essex, Padstow and St Ives in Cornwall, Cardigan and Aberaeron in Wales. In Scotland, branches to Eyemouth and North Berwick, and the coast line along the shores of the Neuk of Fife – the area lying between the firths of Forth and Tay – transformed small ports and fishing harbours.

At times railway companies themselves directly promoted coastal development. Acting through directors and senior company officials, the Stockton & Darlington Railway created Saltburn, including building a prominent hotel next to the

At Cleethorpes the sea front was owned and developed by the Manchester, Sheffield & Lincolnshire (later Great Central) Railway.

From an old postcard

station and laying out gardens. Withernsea was created by the Hull & Holderness Railway, which in 1855 offered free season tickets to prospective commuters to Hull in an endeavour to encourage housing development – of which more in chapter 5 – while at the same time hoping to create a new resort, although it was not very successful. Through its directors the Scarborough & Whitby Railway played a leading role in planning coastal development at Ravenscar and Robin Hood's Bay. There was limited development at the latter, but Ravenscar failed. On the other hand the Manchester, Sheffield & Lincolnshire's efforts at Cleethorpes were not only successful but very profitable under the railway's direct control. The company built the sea wall and promenade, laid out gardens, purchased the pier and provided a variety of attractions. By 1900 it owned over a mile of foreshore. Two smaller railways were less successful. The Furness Railway bought land at Seascale on the Cumbrian coast but, despite providing gas, a water supply and other services, only a few houses were built. On the English side of the Solway Firth, the Carlisle & Silloth Bay Railway attempted to do the same, laying out a small town at Silloth that financially exhausted it to the extent that a Scottish railway, the North British, had to come to the rescue. Despite being moderately successful, Silloth failed to fully reach expectations, although the small railway-owned port did better.

As its name implies, Morecambe Promenade Station faced the sea front. *1980.*

One of the most ambitious and successful railway-created resorts was Morecambe, where a small local company, the North Western Railway (known as the 'Little' North Western to differentiate it from the large London & North Western), began a harbour project at the village of Poulton-le-Sands, population 500, on Morecambe Bay, opening a station and a hotel in 1848. The company soon

came under Midland Railway control, which bought it out in 1871. The Midland quickly began direct train services from West Yorkshire and Poulton soon became a popular resort, renamed Morecambe and tripling its population within five years. By 1900 it was 11,800 and by 1931 over 21,000. The Midland actively assisted growth, building a sea wall and a stone pier from which for a few years it operated steamer services to Belfast. In 1933 the London Midland & Scottish Railway rebuilt the Midland Hotel in classic art deco style, making it a noted seafront landmark. But the harbour scheme never really developed, and instead in 1904 the Midland opened a large new deep-water harbour nearby at Heysham. Curiously, the London & North Western Railway, whose West Coast main line was only 2 miles away, was slow off the mark and did not open a branch to Morecambe until 1864.

Railway ports

By definition, the growth of ports drastically changed the coasts and estuaries on which they were located. Collectively, railways became the largest single owner of ports and docks, and at those they did not own they were complementary. Without railways ports could not expand. Several large ports like London, Liverpool and the Bute Docks at Cardiff had their own private railway systems. From the railways' earliest days ports were an important source of traffic and the companies invested heavily

The original station at Penzance, close to the waterfront, harbour and pier, before reconstruction in c1885.

The station at the railway port of Fleetwood after the arrival of a train of excursionists bound for the Isle of Man in the 1930s.

in serving them. The Liverpool & Manchester Railway had a branch to Liverpool docks from its opening in 1830, and the first line to London's docks dated from 1840, as did the first at Cardiff. The first railway-owned port was Llanelli, purchased by the Carmarthenshire Railway – a tramroad – in 1802. Other combined railway and dock companies followed in South Wales for handling coal. The Barry Dock & Railway Company, which created from scratch the second largest South Wales port after Cardiff, will be examined in chapter 5. The Felixstowe Railway & Pier Company of 1875, later renamed the Felixstowe Dock & Railway, made Felixstowe a small but fashionable resort, although the port stagnated until the 1960s when it grew into what today is Britain's largest container port and heavily reliant on its rail connection.

We have already seen how Sir Peter Hesketh Fleetwood tried to combine a railway, the Preston & Wyre, with a new port named after him, but with only limited success so that the enterprise had to be finished by others. We have also noted how Peto's Lowestoft Railway & Harbour Company succeeded. In many instances railway companies developed existing ports by purchasing them. Southampton was the largest railway port, bought outright in 1892 by the London & South Western Railway, which immediately began to invest £5 million. Hull was bought by the North Eastern Railway in 1893, which similarly embarked on large-scale

Part of the North Eastern Railway's
dock complex at Hull.

Oban Station, now rebuilt
in red brick, stands on
the quayside used by
shipping services to the
Western Isles. *1982.*

development, jointly with the Hull & Barnsley. Railway ownership at Hartlepool was more complex, involving several companies over a number of years until finally coming under North Eastern unified control in 1865. The Manchester, Sheffield & Lincolnshire company owned Grimsby docks from 1845, at first through a subsidiary, transforming a small, impoverished port of 3,700 people into a town of 75,000 by 1911. In 1904 the same company, now renamed the Great Central, developed a new port a few miles away at Immingham on what was virtually a virgin site on the Humber. The docks on the Firth of Forth at Grangemouth were acquired by the Caledonian Railway when it bought the Forth & Clyde Canal which had built them. Those on the opposite shore at Alloa, Methil and Leven in Fife came under the control of its rival, the North British. There were many more, among them packet stations, or ferry ports as we now call them. Some were railway-owned, such as Folkestone, the first port to be bought by a railway, the South Eastern, in 1844, and Stranraer, bought by a consortium of four railways in 1874. Heysham was built by the Midland Railway from scratch in 1904, as was

The slipway at Granton from where the first train ferry operated across the Firth of Forth to Burntisland, before the building of the Forth Bridge. *2001.*

Parkeston Quay Station and its adjoining hotel were established by the Great Eastern Railway to alleviate congestion at the nearby port of Harwich. *1966.*

Parkestone Quay by the Great Eastern in 1882 to relieve Harwich, 2 miles away. Others, such as Dover and Holyhead, relied almost entirely on the railways serving them.

These are just some of the ports owing their existence to the railway. The wider impact of railways on large towns that were also ports will be considered at length in the next chapter.

Although not a railway-owned port, the London & North Western Railway was the principal user of Holyhead, with its own quays and hotel seen here in 1969.

Chapter 4

TOWNSCAPES

To a great extent, terrain shaped railway routes through the countryside and to a considerable degree they quickly became assimilated into their surroundings. The opposite happened in towns, where the effect of railways on urban landscapes was infinitely more pronounced and long-lasting, eventually becoming an accepted part of the scene. They cut swathes through towns and cities, permanently altering street patterns and attracting broad ribbons of industrial development. Construction created unprecedented upheavals, with prominent and permanent results. The social effects were devastating to displaced inhabitants, who received little or no compensation. As J.R. Kellett put it, 'the Victorian railway was ... the most important single agency in the transformation of the central area of Britain's major cities.' It was equally true in many smaller towns. In a two-way but unequal process, railways heavily influenced, and were influenced by, a town's size, shape, street pattern, growth and character and, as in country districts, land ownership was a major factor in the choice of routes. By 1890 railways owned on average as much as 10 per cent of the central land in large towns.

'Mansfield is remembered by the high arches of the railway viaduct (1875) which rise right in the middle of the town and cut off the parish church from the market place,' wrote Nikolaus Pevsner in the Nottinghamshire volume of his *Buildings of England* series in 1979. Indeed, the most notable features of railways in many towns are viaducts. They not only crossed valleys, but also were a common way of minimising land-take in heavily built-up areas, reducing the need to close off streets, which Parliament was always reluctant to sanction. The cheapest land usually contained low-quality property and, compared with rural areas, less care was taken in a viaduct's appearance. Revenue was obtained by letting out arches to a variety of commercial tenants, frequently for industrial trades. Some became shelters for the homeless. They quickly became insalubrious, so that railway viaducts in towns often became synonymous with mean streets and urban degradation. In recent years, fortunately, there has been considerable improvement.

There are notable exceptions. In valley towns a viaduct is often the most prominent feature, boldly announcing the presence of the railway. One of the best known is at Stockport, partly because it figured in early Victorian condemnations of social conditions in industrial towns and partly because of its sheer size: 161ft high, four tracks wide in bright red brick, and stretching over ¼ mile on twenty-two arches looking down on the centre of the town. Yet today, 170 years after it was built, it is regarded as an integral part of the townscape, is Grade II* listed and like Accrington Viaduct in Lancashire, it is floodlit at night. In 1853, W. White in his *Directory and Gazetteer of Leeds….. and the Whole of the Clothing District of Yorkshire* commented on the dominance in Huddersfield of 'Two stupendous viaducts…. on the north and south sides of the town,' one with forty-five arches 53ft high, and the other with thirty-two reaching a height of 122ft. At nearby Wakefield ninety-nine arches stretch for almost ¾ mile across the city. The lofty Foord Viaduct, soaring over the rooftops of Folkestone, has received perhaps the highest accolade from John Newman in his North and East Kent volume in *The Buildings of England* (1993): 'Without any doubt the most exciting piece of architecture in the town.' Equally, Durham Viaduct is now as much a part of the

A.F. Tait's well-known litho of Stockport in 1848 illustrates the urban degradation that often accompanied railway viaducts in industrial areas.

dramatic townscape as the castle and the cathedral. For some years after the Colne Viaduct at Watford was built in 1837 it was regarded as one of the sights of the town. Elegant balustraded parapets add a particularly graceful touch to the twenty-six tall arches of London Road Viaduct, Brighton (1846), while in its day the nearby Montpelier Bridge of 1841 was likened to a triumphal Roman arch. Both bespeak the good manners of many early railway builders, although the original Montpelier Bridge today contrasts with the work of later builders who defaced one side of it with iron girders to widen the line. At Knaresborough in North Yorkshire, four arches with crenellated piers and parapets cross the gorge of the River Nidd. They have long been regarded as complementary to the old town and the overlooking castle, to the extent of being a favourite subject for picture postcards, despite Pevsner's castigation that they ruin the view. Brighton and Knaresborough, of course, were something of a special case. Paisley, west of Glasgow, clearly was not when, in 1840, twenty-eight arches were built to carry

London Road Viaduct divides the older part of Brighton from more recent development. *1992.*

The grade II listed Wicker Arch in Sheffield is a well-known local landmark. *1990.*

the railway across the town. Set low behind buildings, they are of much lesser quality apart from three arches over a road at one end, in full view and therefore given better treatment. The massive, yet graceful Wicker Arch over a broad street leading out of Sheffield is a city landmark known locally as the Gateway to the Don Valley. In small towns the dominance of a viaduct can be even more pronounced: at Shepton Mallet in Somerset, for instance, where there are two; Tavistock, St Austell and Truro in the West Country; and the handsome Markinch viaduct in Fife, to name a few examples. The viaducts at Shifnal in Shropshire and Mytholmroyd in West Yorkshire both had a station perched at one end, the platforms reached by stairs in a tall entrance building alongside an arch.

From mid-century onward ugly iron bridges increasingly defaced the streets of many British towns, attracting public concern. In 1864 the engineer of London's Metropolitan Board of Works deplored 'those hideous iron girders we now find everywhere crossing our streets.' The provinces fared no better. The Regency elegance of Bath Street in Leamington Spa is despoiled by the Great Western Railway's ugly iron bowstring girder bridge at one end. Originally it was hidden by the slightly less ugly deep iron plate girder bridge of the London & North Western's line alongside, which for many years added insult to injury by glaringly advertising Palethorpes' Sausages. Its demolition in 1966 revealed the GWR bridge in full view, in much the same way as the bowstring bridge that marred the centre of the spa town of Ilkley until it, too, was demolished at about the same time. Even so, some iron bridges can be said to enhance their surroundings. After the Forth and Saltash bridges, one of the best known and most widely admired is Robert Stephenson and T.E. Harrison's High Level Bridge over the Tyne at Newcastle of 1849, carrying road as well as rail, linking the city to Gateshead in a way that had long been needed, the first of five lofty bridges that collectively have become a distinctive landmark. The tall Dean Street arch in Newcastle is a noble masonry accompaniment. For many years the mainly Georgian Foregate Street in Worcester was defaced by an iron plate girder bridge leading to a viaduct across the river. When the Great Western replaced the bridge in 1909, the company was persuaded by the city council to improve its appearance, helped by a contribution to the cost of adding a false arch on each side, surmounted by an equally false decorative parapet carrying the arms of the city, the county and the railway company. Friargate in Derby is a street of similar quality, crossed by the low iron arch of the Great Northern Railway. Although an attempt was made to improve its appearance with heavily decorated ironwork, it effectively blocks the view, decried by some but by others now considered to be part of the historic townscape. A similar attempt was made on the three-span plate girder bridge over Queens Road, Hastings, which was given a touch of classical elegance by tall, fluted Doric iron columns. Perhaps to soften the impact of the railways and junctions that dominate the Gorgie district of Edinburgh, three bridges crossing roads were given special treatment by way of elaborately decorated cast iron work.

Parliament and local authorities' reluctance to authorise the stopping up of streets compelled the builders of some large stations to take existing thoroughfares through dark tunnel-like bridges beneath them. In London Charing Cross, Cannon Street and London Bridge stations have streets running underneath in this way, as do Newcastle Central, Birmingham Snow Hill and Rugby. Attempts were made to mitigate the intrusion with ornamental patterned iron parapets at Middlesbrough Station and Great Ducie Street bridge at Manchester Victoria, both crossing main roads, while the long gloomy tunnel taking one of Glasgow's main shopping streets, Argyle Street, under Central Station is enlivened by the highly ornamental iron-and-glass screen walls of the train shed above.

After bridges and viaducts, goods stations, marshalling yards, engine sheds and sidings made the greatest urban impact as they spread across townscapes. Many goods stations were on the site of a former passenger terminus located outside the central area, made redundant when a new, more convenient station was opened. They steadily expanded, swallowing up greater areas of land than any other railway installation. As

The highly decorated iron Albert Bridge runs beneath Middlesbrough Station. *2001.*

towns expanded to encompass them they became part of the industrial urban scene. The effect of large passenger stations was mixed. There were very handsome stations that not only enhanced cities but attracted quality commercial development near them, changing the local environment. Those with arched iron roofs have been called the cathedrals of their age. Equally there were poor ones, many regarded as a disgrace to their host towns and subjected to prolonged criticism. The manner in which all these features affected individual towns will be considered later in this chapter but, because of its size and unique circumstances, London deserves a closer look.

London

Viaducts predominate south of the Thames and in the East End. London's first railway, the London & Greenwich of 1836-38, ran entirely on a viaduct 3¾ miles long. Progressively it was widened to carry twelve tracks from London Bridge station for nearly 2 miles to a maze of junctions at New Cross, cutting a broad swathe across a crowded townscape. Other lines in the south London complex are also on arches, while an even more complicated web of connecting lines and junctions occupies much of Battersea. In the East End, the London & Blackwall and Eastern Counties railways ran on viaducts to their respective termini on the fringe of the City, each over 2 miles long, together with connecting lines. The North London Railway's elevated line into Broad Street was of similar length. Charles Booth, writing in 1892 about the London & South Western's viaduct to Waterloo, called the arches 'an evil; impenetrable boundaries of railway lines from Nine Elms to Clapham Junction', causing bottlenecks where they crossed streets. The evil was compounded by large locomotive sheds and workshops at Nine Elms. The Charing Cross Railway Act of 1859 attempted to remedy traffic congestion by stipulating that bridges across streets should have a single uninterrupted span. This meant that they were literally 'wall-to-wall' with no intermediate supports, requiring deep iron lattice girders. J.M. Wilson's *The Imperial Gazetteer of England and Wales* (1866-69) castigated them

as 'ungainly iron tubes', one of which 'crosses the fine new street from Blackfriars into Southwark, utterly spoiling the handsome aspect.' The engineer Sir John Hawkshaw lamented their ugliness but pointed out that without supporting columns there was no alternative.

Lines entering London from the north and west were less obtrusive. The earliest trunk line into London, the London & Birmingham of 1837, lay in a cutting; the Great Northern Railway into King's Cross, the Midland into St Pancras and, at the end of the century, the Great Central into Marylebone, passed through tunnels. The Great Western to Paddington was mainly a surface line. These termini lay in a line along the New Road, now Euston and Marylebone roads, on the north side of a large central district bounded to the south by the Thames. It was an area through which a Royal Commission of 1846 decreed that no railway should be authorised. This and the intense competition between railway companies were the reasons why London had fifteen terminal stations – if Blackfriars is included – unlike many continental and North American cities where one central terminus was used by all. It still has twelve. In time three southern lines were permitted to cross the Thames, but no further than the north bank, the first at Victoria in 1860, followed by Charing Cross in 1864 and Cannon Street in 1866. Also in that year a fourth was allowed to penetrate the prohibited zone from Blackfriars to Farringdon on the Metropolitan Railway, thereby connecting the southern and northern main lines. On the way it crossed Ludgate Hill on an ugly bridge that completely blocked the view of St Paul's Cathedral, ruining one of London's finest streetscapes. In 1990 it was replaced by the new Thameslink line, using a disused tunnel, ending 130 years of desecration. But an only slightly less objectionable violation remains on the south bank where an iron viaduct emerged from London Bridge station immediately alongside Southwark Cathedral. Although not a cathedral when the line was built in 1864, its ancient origins warranted more respect. The current reconstruction of the station still requires an unavoidable viaduct in this sensitive location.

None of the four railway bridges across the Thames can be said to enhance the riverscape, excepting perhaps Blackfriars –

The railway running out from London Bridge Station cuts a broad swathe through Bermondsey, as seen from The Shard. *2015*.

A.J. Lambert

One of J.M. Wilson's 'ungainly iron tubes' crossing Southwark Street near London Bridge Station. *2010.*

the second on this site – although it was not improved when platforms were built along it as part of the reconstruction of Blackfriars Station in 2013, laudable though the solar panels in the canopies are in generating electricity.

In building London's railways, as in other cities, large-scale demolitions, often of slum property, were unavoidable. The 2 mile extension of the London & Southampton Railway from Nine Elms to Waterloo in 1848 took away 700 houses. Building St Pancras station in 1865 required the demolition of 4,000, displacing an estimated 32,000 people. Again we have to turn to Dickens' *Dombey and Son* for the best contemporary description of the upheaval caused by railway construction when the London & Birmingham was being cut through Camden Town. 'The first shock of a great earthquake had, just at that period, rent the whole neighbourhood to its centre. Houses were knocked down; streets broken through and stopped; deep pits and trenches dug; enormous heaps of earth and clay thrown up; buildings that were undermined and shaking, propped up by great beams of wood.'

Some goods stations and warehouses were close to the passenger termini; others, together with engine sheds, yards and sidings were a mile or so out, some rather more, where they steadily expanded to form dominant features, particularly at Stratford, Willesden and Cricklewood. The Midland Railway at St Pancras, had two goods stations. Somerstown was alongside the terminus but, confusingly, St Pancras goods and coal yard was nearly ½ mile out, adjacent to the Great Northern's large King's Cross goods station and coal yard, and the London & North Western's Maiden Lane depot on the North London line, the three forming a broad concentration ½ mile wide. Marylebone and Broad Street each had a large goods station adjacent, Paddington a smaller one. Liverpool Street goods traffic was handled at the much enlarged former passenger terminus at Bishopsgate, and south of the river the one-time passenger stations at Bricklayers Arms and Nine Elms served the same purpose for London Bridge and Waterloo respectively. Bishopsgate by the early 1900s had become one of London's largest goods stations, covering 21 acres on two levels. Most of the main line railways north of the Thames had additional goods and coal yards in the central area, the East End and the docks, often reached over other companies' tracks. Near King's Cross passenger station there was the added noise and atmospheric pollution of a large locomotive depot, the only one close to central London.

With the exception of London Bridge and Waterloo, all London's main termini, to a greater or lesser degree, made a positive visual contribution to their localities in terms of impressive street frontages, added to at King's Cross, St Pancras, Paddington, Cannon Street and the original Charing Cross by high arched roofs. The great Doric Arch of 1838 at Euston was the first and most imposing grand station entrance, 72ft high and at that time one of the tallest buildings in London outside the City, an unsurpassed classical expression of the power and supreme confidence of the railway as the new means of travel that would unite Britain as never before. In 1881 it was hidden by an extension of the Euston Hotel. Its needless demolition in 1968 was an outstanding act of corporate vandalism. The façade of King's Cross is a notable exercise in simple but imposing functionalism, now at last freed of later accretions to reveal its true worth. The main frontages of most of the other stations were formed by railway hotels: Paddington, Liverpool Street, Cannon Street – now replaced by an office block – and Charing Cross. The more modest façade of Marylebone faces its hotel across the street. It took over 40 years to give respectability to the two side-by-side stations at Victoria. Both had the meanest of wooden frontages until a hotel was built in French Renaissance style on the front of the London, Brighton & South Coast Railway's station. Not to be outdone, the rival South Eastern & Chatham company next door replied with a particularly ostentatious French Renaissance-style façade of its own. After both companies became part of the Southern Railway in 1923 the two stations became one. The frontage of London Bridge was something of a hotch-potch due to similarly divided ownership. Waterloo had to wait until 1921 for a grand entrance arch. Unfortunately a viaduct opposite tends to block it off. St Pancras is London's most prominent railway landmark, totally dominating its locality and dwarfing King's Cross next to it. Both the towering High Victorian hotel and the great arched iron trainshed are

St Pancras at sunset, painted by John O'Connor, 1884.

visible from all around. It is seen at its most dramatic when looking down Pentonville Road in the early morning or evening, its spires and towers rising up, as painted at sunset by John O'Connor in 1884. The effect on adjacent areas alongside and behind the termini was sometimes more negative, particularly around King's Cross which became notoriously squalid, but which is now being redeveloped. In the vicinity of Paddington, however, a virtual new town of quiet streets and modest houses sprang up.

Large provincial cities

More so than in the countryside, topography and land ownership patterns were prominent factors in determining railway routes in towns. Compared with the high visual impact of bridges and viaducts, the influence of tunnels in towns was minimal. Some towns have both, as at Huddersfield and Newport in South Wales, for instance, where the stations are approached from one direction over a viaduct and from the other through a tunnel, in the former directly at the platform ends. Glasgow in particular had certain similarities with London on a smaller scale. It is the only other city where railways were the subject of a Royal Commission, set up in 1846 to, 'consider and report upon the advantages or otherwise of a Central Railway Terminus.' Unlike London's Royal Commission it was ineffective, too late to prevent an uncontrolled spread of intensely competitive lines. Also, like London, Glasgow's stations were termini, four of them, around a central core which railways did not cross, albeit a very small one with little more than ¼ mile between Queen Street and Buchanan Street stations on the north side, and Central and St Enoch on the south. On a still smaller scale Bradford had three termini, and still has two, Exchange (now interchange) and Forster Square, facing each other barely 300 yards apart across a few central streets. Several late nineteenth-century proposals for a connecting tunnel or a viaduct came to nothing and today the only link is still a circuitous route via Leeds. Glasgow in this respect fared much better with its City of Glasgow Union Railway which, although

The ironwork of Glasgow Central Station Bridge overshadows Telford's Glasgow Bridge on one side (seen here) and King George V Bridge on the other. *1992.*

not direct, links lines north and south of the city in a sweeping curve around the east side. East-west local railways crossing the north and south sides of the central area, unseen in tunnels, serve a different purpose and do not connect the main lines at the termini. Queen Street station on the north side is approached through a tunnel, like Buchanan Street before it was closed, while the Clyde, like the Thames, formed a southern boundary crossed by bridges leading to Central and St Enoch. Central Station Bridge is a ponderous lattice girder structure dating from 1905 sandwiched between Telford's elegant Glasgow Bridge of 1833, widened in 1874, and the 1924 King George V Bridge, ruining the aspect of both. The Glasgow Union or St Enoch Bridge (1902) is quite handsome, with iron arched spans and battlemented piers in finely executed sandstone. Again, like London, the south bank of the river borders a linear pattern of sprawling lines and junctions that attracted slum housing and industrial development, including two large goods stations, all forming a barrier. In the 4 miles of suburbia between Ibrox and Polmadie only seven bridges link the areas on either side of the railway. As a final analogy with

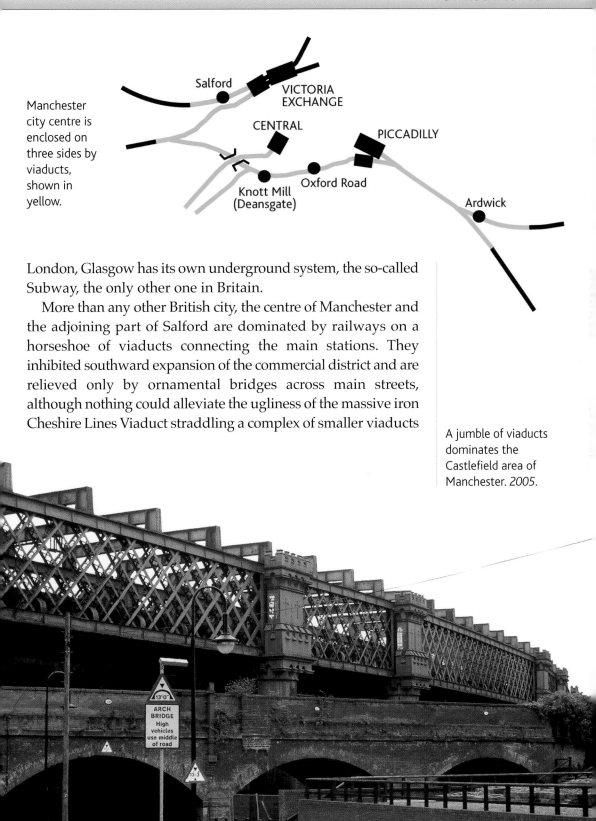

Salford

VICTORIA
EXCHANGE

CENTRAL

PICCADILLY

Knott Mill
(Deansgate)

Oxford Road

Ardwick

Manchester city centre is enclosed on three sides by viaducts, shown in yellow.

London, Glasgow has its own underground system, the so-called Subway, the only other one in Britain.

More than any other British city, the centre of Manchester and the adjoining part of Salford are dominated by railways on a horseshoe of viaducts connecting the main stations. They inhibited southward expansion of the commercial district and are relieved only by ornamental bridges across main streets, although nothing could alleviate the ugliness of the massive iron Cheshire Lines Viaduct straddling a complex of smaller viaducts

A jumble of viaducts dominates the Castlefield area of Manchester. *2005.*

13'0"

ARCH
BRIDGE
High
vehicles
use middle
of road

and canals at Castlefield. The city was a magnet for railway promoters, and the council's efforts to persuade competing companies to join in a single central station failed. Eventually there were four. Similar efforts by the Liverpool municipality and other cities were equally fruitless in the face of a combination of fiercely competing companies, local politics, powerful vested interests and, in Liverpool, the high cost of tunnelling.

The Leeds city authorities, aided by public opinion, fared better. For eleven years after 1840 the town had a handsome station in the terminus of the North Midland Railway, designed by the architect Francis Thompson, but it lay beyond the centre in Hunslet Lane and in 1851 was relegated to a goods station. Thereafter four squabbling companies at first used three stations, then two, none of any merit. In the 1860s the efforts of the North Eastern Railway to build a line across newly laid out streets to a station of its own were vigorously opposed. The company was forced to adopt a more southerly course on a mile-long viaduct to a new, third station, owned jointly with the London & North Western and unimaginatively called Leeds New. Even then the

'The Dark Arches' beneath Leeds Station. The railings line a bridge over the River Aire. *1991.*

railway cut off the ancient parish church from the town, running across part of the graveyard on an embankment on which displaced gravestones were re-laid. The station was built on a viaduct, five platforms and nine tracks wide at a point where it spanned the River Aire, requiring a broad and complicated pattern of vaulted brick cross-arches which were let to tenants. A spine road running down the centre underneath the station gave access to side arches and included a bridge across the river and an arm from the adjacent Leeds & Liverpool Canal. They became known as the Dark Arches and quickly gained an unsavoury reputation. According to a police report of 1892 they were a centre of 'idling loose women' and muggings, and even formed the subject of a popular song in Leeds pubs and taverns about a man being lured into them by a pretty girl, robbed and left naked in the gutter. Today, cleaned and imaginatively lit, they have been transformed into an arts centre and craft workshops. It was 1967, on the closure of the unlamented Leeds Central, before the city at last enjoyed a single station.

Topography usually dictated tunnel approaches. Because Birmingham is situated on a hill, the London & Birmingham and Grand Junction railways terminated short of the city. When their successor, the London & North Western, and its rival the Great Western wanted to extend northward through the town they could only do so by tunnelling. Consequently Birmingham's two stations are the most centrally sited in any large British city. Snow Hill on the Great Western is entered from the south through a tunnel and leaves on a viaduct followed by a tunnel. The other, larger station, New Street, is entered at both ends through tunnels. In fact, the city itself ensured that the station was deliberately hidden. The authorising Act required high brick walls and parapets on the bridges at each end, and the street commissioners stipulated that the platforms must be completely roofed over. Moreover, goods trains were prohibited from passing through the station, an alternative route being available, and engines were not to stand in the station any longer than necessary, a requirement that often was ignored. The commissioners appear to have had a hand in the southern approach tunnel to Snow Hill, too. The end nearest to the station was intended to be an open cutting, but the commissioners insisted on its being roofed over, and a shopping arcade was built on it. In the building of both stations the city also gained street improvements, while at New Street a large area of slum property was cleared. There are other towns where tunnels similarly avoid intrusion by leading directly into the station: Chatham and Tunbridge Wells Central for instance, in the latter case particularly important in a spa town.

Topography strongly influenced the rail approaches to Liverpool from the east which, in order to overcome a steep descent, meant that acceptable gradients could only be achieved by tunnelling. The city was the gainer, avoiding permanent disruption. The lines to the first station at Crown Street and a branch to the docks were in tunnels. Crown Street's successor, Lime Street, and Central station also had steep tunnel approaches. When additional tracks were needed, part of Lime Street tunnel was opened out into a deep, narrow rock cutting that, were it not for sound and smoke, was hardly more obtrusive. Only Exchange station, approached more easily from the north, had an elevated approach on a low viaduct close to the riverside dock road. Even that was largely hidden from the centre of town. The most intrusive of the city's lines was the Liverpool Overhead Railway, extending for 6½ miles along the waterfront on an iron viaduct. The first elevated electric railway in the world, it was for long a notable feature of the city, although it has to be said that after it closed in 1956 the view of the city's imposing and well-known Pierhead buildings was immeasurably improved. Liverpool cannot be left without mentioning an unusual feature on the Edge Hill–Bootle branch at Anfield, where the railway borders Liverpool cemetery, crossing the entrance from Cherry Lane at an acute angle on a remarkably elaborate tunnel-like bridge that doubles up as a grand Gothic gateway, dated 1864 and replete with turrets, coats of arms, other insignia and decorative wrought-iron gates.

When in the late 1900s the Manchester, Sheffield & Lincolnshire Railway cut through Nottingham and Leicester in building its new main line to London, it provided stations more centrally located than those of the incumbent, the Midland Railway, but

only at the expense of a tunnel beneath the heart of Nottingham followed by a viaduct, and in Leicester a mile-long viaduct after being compelled to avoid important Roman and medieval sites. The early Dundee & Newtyle Railway of 1831 tunnelled under Dundee Law in order to achieve a direct line into the city from the north, virtually through the streets, but when an easier route replaced it in 1861, a more indirect one was chosen around the eastern side. The later main lines from the south and northward to Aberdeen kept to the edge of Dundee along the waterfront, aiding the growth of the port but completely changing the shore in the process. The civic authorities at Southampton ensured that the first railway to the city terminated just outside the walls by providing cheap land, while later lines to the extended docks almost encircled the old town but did not cross it, a tunnel being necessary to take the line to Dorchester and the west. As a result a station on it had to be located outside the town at Blechynden, later renamed Southampton West, and later still, on a slightly different site, Southampton Central which, following the expansion of the town westward, it was now considered to be.

Port traffic strongly influenced rail routes in Cardiff, an old town that in the century following 1830 grew from less than

This elaborate structure doubles up as a bridge carrying Liverpool's Edge Hill–Bootle branch and the entrance to the cemetery at Anfield. 2013.

The Taff Vale
Railway's
headquarter offices
at Cardiff stood
alongside Queen
Street Station, now
rebuilt. *1971.*
Gordon Rattenbury

2,000 people to a city of over 200,000 dominated by railways and docks for the export of coal. The South Wales Railway (later part of the GWR) was first on the scene, running from east to west along the south side of the town, with a station on land reclaimed by diverting the River Taff. On the east and west sides it was followed by the lines of the Taff Vale Railway, bringing coal down from the valleys of Glamorgan to the north. The line on the east side was joined by the Rhymney Railway. None of them penetrated the old town, which rapidly expanded to envelop them. The chief monument was the Taff Vale's extravagant French-Gothic Queen Street station and headquarters building, completely outclassing the Great Western's wooden 'Brunel Barn' until it was rebuilt more appropriately for Wales's largest city in 1880 and again in 1932. Swansea's docks equally influenced railway construction, but because of its location at the foot of a narrow valley, the city suffered from being served by what in effect were branch lines running down each side, always a source of grievance, none of them penetrating the centre. At one time there were six termini, later reduced to three and now one.

Railways at a third large port, Hull, made a quite different impact. The flat terrain meant that level crossings were the only practicable way of crossing streets. Within the city boundary there were thirteen, long the subject of complaints about delays to road traffic. A similar problem afflicted the centre of Lincoln, which had four level crossings in a small area, two of them only 200 yards apart across the High Street. Latterly one of the four has been replaced by a bridge and another one closed, but the present High Street crossing still arouses concern. Burton-upon-Trent, too, was bedevilled by level crossings, not just on main lines, but on busy mineral lines serving the town's many breweries, most of them ungated.

The primary purpose of serving docks influenced railway development at Plymouth, culminating in an elongated horseshoe of lines on which all of the city's three stations were over ½ mile from the centre, despite several civic efforts to gain a central station. At Bristol the topography dissuaded the Great Western Railway in 1840 from building Temple Meads Station nearer the city centre than almost a mile, an inconvenience it has suffered from ever since, while it had to wait until 1874 before a branch was built to the harbour. On the other hand, both cities were spared railways through their historic cores.

During the earlier years of railway construction, choosing the easiest or most direct route was often the prime consideration, resulting in a number of important places being bypassed and undergoing the inconvenience of a station well outside the town or, worse, on a branch line. Sometimes thirty years or more elapsed before a rival company provided something better, usually at the expense of having to cut through areas that in the meantime had become heavily built up, as we have seen at Leicester and Nottingham. Exeter suffered in this way. The Bristol & Exeter Railway opened to the city in 1844 and two years later the South Devon continued on towards Plymouth. Both became part of the Great Western. They kept to the valley of the Exe, with a station at St Davids at the bottom of a hill nearly a mile from the city centre. It was left to the London & South Western in 1876 to provide a more central station in Queen Street, requiring expensive cuttings, overbridges and a tunnel. Sheffield suffered much worse. In 1840 the North Midland, later the Midland Railway, routed its south-to-north main line as much as 4 miles away from the rapidly-growing town, leaving it on a branch from Rotherham. In 1849 the situation was improved for west-to-east services by the completion of the Manchester, Sheffield & Lincolnshire Railway through the north side of the town on a viaduct, with a station at one end. But it was 1870 before continual civic pressure persuaded the Midland to build a direct line through the city, by which time it had greatly expanded to the extent that the new railway needed expensive stone-lined cuttings, fifteen bridges in less than a mile, a large tract of built-up land for a station and the compulsory purchase of over 1,000 houses, many of them new. Even then, neither of the stations could be called central.

For nearly twenty years Aberdeen had to tolerate two unconnected terminal stations 1½ miles apart, one at the end of a viaduct entering the city from the south and the other coming down the Denburn Valley from the north to the quayside. Through passengers had to cross the town on foot or by cab. As the two companies refused to co-operate by holding connecting trains in cases of late running by one of them, more often than not connections were missed. Eventually, in 1867, sense prevailed and a through line and a joint central station were built, needing two tunnels. A similar connecting line across Edinburgh between Haymarket and Waverley stations caused four years of bitter controversy. The only practicable route lay along the narrow valley between the Old and New Towns, overlooked by the castle. As it had recently been laid out as gardens the proposal aroused strong feelings, and it was only after the Edinburgh & Glasgow Railway agreed to provide extensive landscaping and screening with trees that the line was permitted. It was opened in 1846 and included a tunnel beneath the Scottish National Gallery on The Mound. Later, more controversy arose over widening the line and demolition of

ancient buildings to make way for enlargements to Waverley. The burghers of Perth were more successful. When, in 1845, four railways proposed to establish a joint station on the South Inch, a treasured expanse of riverside parkland granted to the city by Royal Charter, there were loud protests and adjudicators were appointed. They gave their approval, subject to screening by trees and to the station being 'of highly ornamental character', but their decision was roundly rejected by the town, forcing the companies to take a more expensive route and an awkward station layout that still exists today.

In 1882-83 the citizens of Norwich were equally successful in rejecting a proposal for a railway across the Lower Close of the cathedral. Leamington Spa attempted to avoid railway intrusions by gaining special clauses in the Great Western's Act of 1848, protecting newly laid out streets, parks and avenues, specifying minimum distances from important buildings, and maximum dimensions and screening of bridges. As we have seen, the Great Western got away with building a bowstring girder bridge, perhaps because it was hidden by the slightly less

Edinburgh Waverley Station and the tunnels under The Mound, from Calton Hill. *1992.*

The termination of Regency Bath Street, Leamington Spa, is spoiled by the Great Western Railway bridge. 1992.

objectionable London & North Western company's bridge alongside, which was already there. Engines, carriages and the interior of the station had to be screened 'for ever'. The Great Western's response in 1852 was to build a slightly superior version of one of its wooden roofed barn-like stations. The LNWR station of 1851 also was wooden but was regarded as temporary. Described locally as 'wretched', it lasted until 1860 when it was replaced in a seemly Italianate style on a broad crescent approach road, much more in keeping with the town.

Conversely, in 1840-44, the Great Western and I.K. Brunel appear to have gone to great lengths to respect Georgian Bath. The eastern approaches pass beneath handsome elliptically-arched bridges, and traverse Sydney Gardens in a cutting lined with elegantly curved walls, all in carefully dressed ashlar masonry. Unfortunately Brunel's successors extensively refaced St James's Bridge over the river in brick, leaving only patches of stone. Further on, his fine laminated timber-arched Avon

Bridge had decorative ironwork within its spandrels. It was replaced by a latticed wrought-iron girder bridge in 1878, modified in 1959. It is followed by St James's Viaduct, a series of segmental masonry arches, again unfeelingly patched in brick. At Southgate Bridge the style changes to Tudor-Gothic, complete with buttresses and turrets, possibly out of respect to the former medieval street and nearby Bath Abbey, but suffering from later road widening when pointed stone arches were replaced by steel girders rather incongruously topped by crenellated stone parapets. Tudor styling is resumed on Twerton Viaduct, station and tunnels. Equal care was taken with the city's two main stations, the GWR's in Jacobean style and the Midland's splendidly classical.

I.K. Brunel's carefully engineered bridges and cutting through Sydney Gardens, Bath. *1984.*

Railway violations

The despoiling of Ludgate Hill in London was not the only example of urban violation. York's city walls were breached in order to let the York & North Midland Railway into a central terminus, something that would be unthinkable today, albeit that the damage was partly ameliorated by well-designed

The first railway to York entered through this arch cut in the ancient city wall. *1991.*

arches by a good architect, subject to the approval of the Yorkshire Philosophical Society and leading to a handsome station. It was no coincidence that the company's chairman, the railway tycoon George Hudson, shortly became Lord Mayor of York. In much the same way the Chester & Holyhead Railway cut through the city walls at Chester and Conwy, fairly respectably, although when the line was widened through Chester the stone arch was replaced by battlemented plate girders in much the same manner as at Bath. Newcastle fared much worse. The York, Newcastle & Berwick Railway cut the castle in two with what Pevsner called 'ruthlessness', separating the twelfth-century keep from the thirteenth-century Black Gate, a price obviously felt worth paying in order to have a station in a central location. Building the station itself also required demolition of some historic property. With equal disregard, the London, Brighton & South Coast Railway cut through St Pancras Priory at Lewes. At Berwick-upon-Tweed the North British Railway compounded injury by using some of the stone from the demolished castle to build a mock-Gothic station on the site. In 1859 the castle ruins at Northampton were, to quote Pevsner again, 'obliterated by the railway', the London

& North Western, to make way for a station which, with unfeeling irony, it named Northampton Castle. When compared with John Livock's fine 1845 neo-Tudor Bridge Street Station on the same company's Peterborough line, now gone, the contrast could not have been greater.

The medieval university in central Glasgow was demolished in 1871 to make way for the large College and High Street goods stations. Admittedly the buildings were in a poor state in what had become a notorious slum area, but nevertheless such vandalism would not be tolerated today. Worse, in the Saltmarket a heavy latticed girder bridge obstructs the view of two of Glasgow's oldest buildings, the 1626 Tolbooth Steeple and the 1665 Merchants' Steeple, while similar bridges form the background to the view of Glasgow Cross from Trongate. Pevsner called the railway's passage through Shrewsbury 'callous'. Actually, it provided two extraordinary contrasts. In 1849 the fine view along the Severn was interrupted by a stone-

The view of one of Glasgow's oldest buildings, the 1626 Tolbooth Steeple, is obstructed by a bridge on the Glasgow & South Western Railway. *1992.*

arched railway bridge that itself was quite handsome, until in 1890-1904 the masonry on both sides was hidden by bleak ironwork carrying an extension of the station out over the river. Yet the station's very fine neo-Tudor frontage that had been built to harmonise with the nearby sixteenth-century Shrewsbury School was admirably enlarged in 1903, barely distinguishable from the original, but spoiled by a glaring red brick retaining wall beneath the medieval castle mound facing it.

Large provincial stations

The effect of railways on towns was by no means always negative. Many were provided with a handsome station that was regarded with pride along with the town hall and other civic and important commercial buildings that characterised the growth of Victorian cities. The stations themselves frequently attracted street improvements. The London & Birmingham's immense Doric Arch at Euston of 1838 was matched at the other end of the line by the classical Ionic entrance to Curzon Street station in Birmingham, fortunately still standing. Both contrasted with the draughty open-sided iron-and-glass sheds in which passengers boarded trains. Other monumental stations followed throughout the nineteenth century, their infinite variety reflecting the changes in Victorian architectural fashion: Palladian at Southampton Terminus, the original Paragon station building at Hull, and at Brighton, this last on a man-made plateau high on the hillside overlooking the town. The original Dundee West was boldly Italianate, and its successor equally bold Scottish Baronial, both now gone. The first Liverpool Lime Street station, Glasgow Bridge Street and Leicester Campbell Street were classical, all also gone. There is a surprisingly massive classical station at Monkwearmouth, across the river from Sunderland, only surpassed by the large and imposing frontage to Newcastle Central and the immensely long façade at Huddersfield, Britain's finest classical station. Gothic, Tudor and Jacobean were equally popular in providing elaborate display to symbolise the railway revolution: Bristol Temple Meads, Carlisle, Perth, Middlesbrough and an elaborate French Gothic version at Cardiff Queen Street.

Above all stands the supreme example of Victorian High Gothic taste at St Pancras.

In some large towns an imposing station frontage was often formed by a railway hotel, as we have seen in London. Hotels formed an integral part of the stations at Birmingham New Street and Snow Hill, Liverpool Lime Street and Exchange, three Glasgow stations – Central, Queen Street and St Enoch – Edinburgh Princes Street, and Hull Paragon, among others. As in London, some were separate buildings, such as Edinburgh Waverley where one of the city's notable landmarks is the North British Hotel – now renamed the Balmoral – York, Sheffield Victoria, Perth, Manchester Central and Southampton. Their high standards made them popular venues for civic and commercial functions. Possessing a railway hotel became a town's status symbol.

From the 1850s onward, station rebuilding and enlargement introduced a new prominent feature in many townscapes. Great arched iron roofs began to replace the earlier low trainsheds. Progressively they became wider and higher, towering above nearby buildings, sometimes rising above the station frontage building itself to become the dominant feature, as happened at

The centre of Huddersfield is enhanced by its very fine classical station. *1972.*

City Road, Chester, was built to connect the town to the station, seen in the distance. *1992.*

Brighton, and at Liverpool Lime Street until the North Western Hotel partly obscured it. Pride of place again has to go to St Pancras, where for a time the roof was the widest and highest in the world. These arched trainsheds came to epitomise the great city station, the pride of the railway and a mark of a town's importance. Not everyone was impressed. *The Engineer* in 1868 objected to the 'great rotundity' of St Pancras, where 'height appears to be the object aimed at.'

With the coming of the railway a number of towns, large and small, benefited from a new street leading to the station, prompting property development. Several have already been noticed. Others such as Queens Road at Brighton – to which the railway contributed £2,000 and a new bridge – City Road at Chester, Prince of Wales Road in Norwich and Eaton Road at Coventry were built to improve access to stations which at the time were outside the town. The opposite happened at Derby, where the municipality insisted on the station being kept out of town, in return undertaking to build a new road to it. Birmingham considered building a new street to Curzon Street Station, but thought better of it, which was just as well as the station became redundant when only a few years later the railway was extended into the city. Cambridge suffered from having its station a mile away, reached by a new street appropriately called Station Road. Newcastle Central Station was intended to be the major feature at the bottom of Grainger Street, the main thoroughfare in the new city centre planned by Richard Grainger and the architect John Dobson. Most of it was completed as intended, apart from a short length at the foot of the new street which was extended later on a slightly different alignment. As a consequence it just misses making the grand portico of the station a satisfying completion to the vista. At Bath, on the other hand, Brunel deliberately offset the centre of his station's façade to align it with the end of Manvers Street, a new road that the Great Western was obliged to construct under its Act of Incorporation.

Fine stations rarely act as a focal point in the layout of city centres in the way they do in Europe and North America, where

Dundee enjoyed the fine Scottish Baronial style of its West Station from 1889 until its closure in 1969.

Dundee & District Libraries

often they are the focus of a square or other large public space. The Euston arch was fronted by gardens until a railway hotel blocked it from view, while its Birmingham counterpart at Curzon Street was located in an area of mean streets, canal wharves and, later, goods yards, which until recent years it still was. Turning again to Huddersfield, the town fared much better thanks to the strict control of the trustees of the Ramsden Estates, who were laying out new streets. In 1844 Friedrich Engels in *The Condition of the Working Class in England* called it 'the handsomest by far of all the factory towns of Yorkshire and Lancashire', and three years later the trustees not only strongly influenced the design of the station but built a square in front of it, appropriately setting off what many today consider to be Huddersfield's finest building. On the extension of the Liverpool & Manchester Railway into Lime Street the Liverpool city council ensured that the station was in keeping with the square it was creating by contributing £2,000 to the cost of a classical façade designed by its own architect. Later the concept was rather impaired when the facade was replaced by the massive North Western Hotel, which itself became a Liverpool landmark. Surprisingly, in a town not noted for architectural merit, Blackburn station faces a quite spacious triangular 'square' alongside what is now the cathedral, while at Carlisle the city was improved by demolishing a gas works, marble works and some slum property in order to lay out a small square in front of William Tite's richly Tudor-Gothic station that he designed to complement Sydney Smirke's Citadel lawcourts opposite. More modestly, Forster Square at Bradford fronts the station bearing its name.

Leeds laid out City Square in the 1890s to mark its incorporation as a city, but neither of the two stations facing it did it justice. The Midland Railway's Wellington station had a nondescript wooden front that fortunately was masked by the company's Queens Hotel. The London & North Western and North Eastern companies' joint Leeds New station had a spacious glass-and-iron trainshed but no sort of frontage at all. The third Leeds station nearby, Central, occupied by four companies, was no better: a low dark shed fronted by a meagre brick building. Not until 1938 did Leeds get a station worthy of the city and its square when Wellington and New were combined and renamed Leeds City, fronted by a new Queens Hotel in art deco-classical style that more than made up for former shortcomings. Few mourned the demolition of Central after it closed in 1967. The only public square that was a true railway creation is at Stoke-on-Trent, where the North Staffordshire Railway deliberately created a complete entity in Winton Square. The station's rich Jacobean façade is complemented by the company's North Staffordshire Hotel opposite, with matching houses for senior railway officials along the sides. A smaller square fronts Inverness station, with the handsome Highland Railway headquarters on one side and the Station Hotel on the other, but spoiled by the insipid 1960s rebuilt station frontage. Tite's Southampton terminus is set off by a spacious street, but Brunel's Temple Meads station at Bristol fronted a street at the end of a somewhat tortuous route from the city. It had to wait thirty years for more direct access, enlargement, and a worthy approach road to Matthew Digby Wyatt's new French-Gothic entrance building.

Leeds was not the only city which could be said to have been debased by its railway stations. For many years the Great

Unveiling the Cameron Statue in Station Square, Inverness, in 1893. The Highland Railway's offices are on the left, and its Royal Station Hotel opposite.

Courtesy A.J. Lambert

OPENING OF THE SOUTH DEVON RAILWAY AT PLYMOUTH.

The opening of the South Devon Railway at Plymouth Millbay in 1849. The trainshed is a typical wooden 'Brunel Barn'.

Western was notorious for its wooden stations, contrasting so vividly with Brunel's masterpieces at Bristol and Paddington. Basically a mean wooden shed, they came in various sizes. Surprisingly, they were extraordinarily long-lived. Despite many years of public demands for something better than 'Brunel's Barns' as they were called, they continued to disgrace important towns like Cardiff, Newport, Swansea and Plymouth (where there were two) into the 1920s and '30s. Exeter was more fortunate in gaining a replacement at St Davids as early as 1864. Smaller ones also lasted a long time, but today there is only one left, Frome in Somerset, listed for its historical value.

In 1888 an opportunity to create an impression was missed at Bradford when the Lancashire & Yorkshire Railway opened its new Exchange station, also used by the Great Northern. The lack of any kind of external presence was a complete anti-climax to the impressive twin-arched roof. The head of the station was approached by narrow stairs sandwiched between commercial buildings which entirely hid it, while the so-called main entrance was merely a broad opening in a side of the trainshed

The main entrance to Bradford Exchange was merely an opening in the side of the trainshed, contrasting strongly with the imposing arched roof. *1946*.

The landmark arched roof at Manchester Central, seen here in 1964, fortunately has survived as an exhibition hall.
Manchester Public Libraries

wall, tucked away behind the Great Northern Hotel. The entrance to the Midland's Forster Square Station, although fairly modest, certainly was more imposing, although somewhat overpowered by the Midland Hotel alongside. Manchester Central's fine arched roof, second only to St Pancras, also suffered from lack of a decent frontage. What there was comprised low wooden buildings intended to be temporary, but which became permanent. The Midland Hotel was meant to replace them, and an illustration was published, but instead one was built on a detached site connected to the station by a covered way. Unlike Bradford Exchange there was a credit side in that the great roof was left fully exposed, to become a noted Manchester landmark today.

Glasgow could boast three imposing stations. A fourth, Buchanan Street, was a wretched wooden place. It was rebuilt in 1932, again in timber, but slightly more respectably with second-hand platform canopies recovered from Ardrossan. The frontage of the North British Railway's Edinburgh Waverley also was unimpressive, at the foot of an approach slope from Waverley Bridge or, for pedestrians, at the bottom of Waverley Steps alongside the North British Hotel. Internally the station was a model of convenience beneath a broad, airy ridge-and-furrow glass roof. The entrance to the Caledonian Railway's Princes Street station was not quite as modest but it, like Waverley, was overshadowed by a large railway hotel, the Caledonian.

Smaller towns

The railway through Stamford was welcomed, but not at the price of spoiling the town and the Marquis of Exeter's view from Burleigh House. So in 1848 it was taken along one side in a cutting with a short cut-and-cover tunnel at the most sensitive point. Additionally, the Midland Railway paid £5,000 towards widening the River Welland bridge leading to a seemly station, giving the town a double victory. Stamford's other station, the Great Northern's opened in 1856, was equally in keeping with the character of the town. In local grey limestone, the Tudor

The modest Gothic style of Stamford Town station, in local stone, attunes well with its surroundings. *1993.*

styling of both blended easily into the townscape yet was sufficiently distinctive to advertise their presence. Were it not for the marquis's renewed opposition, Stamford might have found itself on the Great Northern's main line instead of on a branch. Instead the GNR chose an easier route through Peterborough, to that town's great commercial benefit. Likewise, in 1844 Abingdon, then the county town of Berkshire with a population of 4,000, lost out when the Great Western Railway chose to avoid the town by 3 miles on an equally easy route to Oxford, rather than face trouble from an obstructive landowner. As a result Abingdon had to wait twelve years to get a locally-promoted branch line.

Stamford was one of a goodly number of historic towns where care was taken to erect a station that respected the local environment. Louth station, also in Lincolnshire, possessed considerable Jacobean charm. Conwy, Melrose, and the original building at Thetford were equally at ease in a similar style; Gravesend and Canterbury West were quietly classical; Winchester had Regency overtones. The station at Letchworth was well in tune with the Arts and Crafts character of the first garden city. Stone and Tamworth in Staffordshire were more opulently Jacobean, although not obtrusively so. At Paisley, the crenellated parapets and turrets of Gilmour Street station sat comfortably along one side of County Square between the earlier county buildings, now demolished, and the later post office, forming a satisfying entity, while further north a modest Scottish Baronial style made Aboyne and Elgin stations perfectly at home.

This respect for historic towns was mainly confined to the years 1840-60 and extended to a measure of larger market and county towns as well. The stations at Lincoln, Durham, Lancaster and the first one at Lewes, for example, all fitted comfortably into their localities. The neo-classical station at Lewes was closed as long ago as 1857, yet lasted until the 1970s when, sadly, it failed to survive redevelopment. It was in the 1840s that two fiercely competing railways, the Great Western and the London & South Western, fought to build branches to Windsor, not only fighting between themselves but against powerful local opposition from Eton College and the Crown. The town council was divided. The railways won, but only at the price of huge contributions to new streets, bridges and other improvements to the town and the castle's Great Park: £25,000 from the Great Western and £60,000 from the LSW, amounting in present-day terms to several millions apiece. The South Western Company also built a handsome station with a Royal suite. By contrast the Great Western's was one of Brunel's customary wooden-roofed 'barns' with a few embellishments. It lasted until 1897 when it was rebuilt in a more appropriate manner to mark Queen Victoria's diamond jubilee, with an imposing entrance arch and a Royal waiting room, although incorporating many of the company's standard features of that time.

Not all new roads to stations were built on the initiative of the local authority. Acts authorising the building of a railway sometimes stipulated that a road should be built to a station, as we have already seen at Bath. The 'Little' North Western Railway was compelled by its Act to provide the small town of Settle in North Yorkshire with a new road to shorten the distance to the nearest station at Giggleswick. Later, Settle had its own station on the Settle & Carlisle line. At Richmond in the same county, a similar requirement included an expensive four-arched bridge over the River Swale. Even greater expense was incurred by the London & North Western Railway in 1900 in

building ½ mile of new road to Cleckheaton station, West Yorkshire, including an iron trestle viaduct 130 yards long crossing the valley from the town. At Cockermouth in Cumbria a local new street company was formed to provide easier access to the station.

Because they were at important junctions, some stations were larger than the size of the town at that time warranted. Shrewsbury, Carlisle, Chester and York, for instance, were at the junction of several lines, resulting in some notable stations that gave prestige to both town and railway. Later on, with changes in taste some ostentation appeared, as at Exeter St Davids and Norwich. The third and final station at Lewes was in a particularly florid style favoured by the London, Brighton & South Coast Railway at that time. The depths of mediocrity were reached at Oxford where for over 120 years the Great Western's mean wooden station was a disgrace, long complained about by town and gown, but not demolished until 1973 when it was replaced by an only slightly better

The grand red-brick Gothic of Windsor & Eton Riverside station, 1851, was built to accommodate Queen Victoria and her entourage on visits to the castle. *1984.*

The end-screens at Buxton's twin stations were made to match at the behest of the Duke of Devonshire, who owned most of the town. *1953.*

prefabricated structure that lasted for fewer than ten years before a more permanent station was built, modern but respectful of a venerable university city, now again replaced.

Spa towns were affected more by a railway increasing their popularity, promoting subsequent growth, than by its physical presence. Buxton and Great Malvern had handsome stations, the former a side-by-side pair with matching decorative screen walls, embellishments added at the insistence of the Duke of Devonshire, who owned most of Buxton. Great Malvern Station was designed as the focal point of a set piece comprising gardens, a pair of bridges, and an overlooking hotel – not railway owned – all by the same architect. Harrogate station, on the other hand, was unremarkable, although it attracted quality commercial development that grew into a new town centre, while the railway made a special effort to keep its line across the large and greatly valued open space of The Stray as unobtrusive as possible in a stone-lined cutting. Railways skirted round the fashionable quarter of Cheltenham. Only one of its three stations, the small terminus of St James, penetrated the central area. In northern Scotland, the Highland Railway's

Kyle line was compelled by a landowner to avoid Strathpeffer, forcing the spa town to be content with a branch line. There the dominant feature was not the railway itself but the company's Highland Hotel.

Just as in large towns, so at a small one the coming of a railway could bring unwelcome new development, particularly where the station was outside it and the area between became in-filled with less-than-harmonious buildings. At Ely, for instance, the dignified station was designed by a sensitive architect, Francis Thompson, in 1845, but during the ensuing years the road into the town became the focus of poor quality housing that in the 1860s was described as an area of squalid property that contrasted with the splendid cathedral.

Later, as often as not disharmony was the result of a policy of standardisation in station design. The Great Eastern Railway

Since this photograph was taken of the picturesque station at Great Malvern in 1962 the tower and spire have been removed. The surrounding gardens and approach road were laid out at the same time as the station in 1860.

was early in the field from about 1865, resulting in near-identical buff and red brick stations in differing areas, for example at Braintree in Essex, Lavenham and Clare in Suffolk. As referred to in chapter 2, the Midland Railway adopted the same corporate policy, but generally with some care taken to use appropriate local materials. Conversely, from the 1880s the Great Western's corporate red brick designs appeared regardless all over its system, at locations as diverse as Truro, Gloucester, Bicester, Warwick and Droitwich. The London & North Western's standard wooden station was equally widespread. The buildings at Uppingham in Rutland and Slaithwaite in West Yorkshire were little different from the suburban stations in north London and south Manchester.

Melrose station reflects Jacobean styling. 1986.

Goods stations and warehouses

After viaducts, the largest and most intrusive railway installations in the inner urban scene were large goods yards. Some of those on the site of an original passenger station that subsequently was moved to a more central location were Crown Street in Liverpool, Oldham Road and Liverpool Road in Manchester, Nine Elms in London, Curzon Street and Lawley Street in Birmingham and St Leonards in Edinburgh. City goods yards expanded enormously to contain huge acreages of sidings, coal depots, transit sheds and warehouses. In the main they were located outside the civic and commercial area, although there were exceptions. As we have seen, Glasgow was a notable one,

The road frontage of the massive goods warehouse at Heaton Norris, Stockport, dominates the locality. *1990*.

like Manchester where the yards at Liverpool Road, Ducie Street and Deansgate had massive multi-storey warehouses, especially the last which is particularly dominant, competing for attention with the great arched roof of Central Station close by and fronting a quarter of a mile of one of the city centre's main thoroughfares. Tall warehouses were a particular feature of many northern English and Scottish textile towns, seven or more storeys high and often prominently displaying their owners' name in indelible white brick, such as those at Bolton, Rochdale and Huddersfield. At Bradford, the Lancashire & Yorkshire Railway's large red brick Bridge Street warehouse challenged the neighbouring Gothic town hall. Generally they were strictly utilitarian buildings, but a few were quite elaborate, like the London & North Western's at Edge Hill, Liverpool, in decorated yellow brick proclaiming 'Fruit and Vegetable Depot, 1881.' This was for special use, along with others such as the series of bonded stores built by the

This Midland Railway grain warehouse was built for the Burton-upon-Trent brewery traffic. *1986*.

Midland Railway for the Burton-upon-Trent brewery traffic, and the enormous Bell Street bonded warehouse and stable block in central Glasgow, part of the College goods station complex. Multi-storey granaries were equally prominent features at some city goods stations, for example King's Cross, Marsh Lane at Leeds, Nottingham London Road and Northampton Bridge Street; also at country towns, like Ware in Hertfordshire for the local maltings, Duns and Eassie in Scotland and, particularly noteworthy, the Midland Railway's at Oakham, alongside a large provender store that provided fodder for the company's several thousand horses.

Liverpool and Plymouth had the distinction of goods depots that were quite devoid of rail tracks. The large, elaborately Italianate Whitechapel goods station in central Liverpool served as a road collection and delivery warehouse for the Midland Railway's nearest goods yard at Sandon Dock. At Plymouth the Great Western's Barbican fish market beside Sutton Harbour,

The Midland Railway's Whitechapel goods station in the centre of Liverpool is not rail served, but acts as a road collection and delivery depot and warehouse. 1996.

built in that company's unmistakable style, had no rail connection, any more than the London & South Western Railway's four-storey goods and parcels receiving depot opposite. Concentrations of goods yards, engine sheds and junctions in some large industrial towns formed what can be called 'railway districts', as we have seen in south London and Glasgow. Some were very large indeed. One of the most extensive was the triangular area on the eastern approaches to Birmingham New Street, a mile long and ½ mile wide, containing lengthy viaducts, two large goods stations and marshalling yards, and a large engine shed. There, railways virtually cut off the suburb of Saltley from the city. An adjoining triangle to the south is dominated on one side by the massive blue brick Bordesley Viaduct, four tracks wide and ¾ mile long, and the South Suburban line on another. It is bisected by yet a third viaduct, Duddeston, built in 1852 to give the Great Western access to the London & North Western Railway's New Street station, but the two companies could not agree so the Great Western built its own station at Snow Hill instead. The viaduct remained unconnected at one end, and was never used: one of the more pointless monuments to early Victorian inter-railway politics. A similar but slightly smaller concentration of railways lay immediately south of the

Like Liverpool Whitechapel, the Great Western's depot in Plymouth's Barbican had no rail access, but was built alongside Sutton Harbour for fish traffic. *1991*.

Brooklands station on Britain's first suburban line, the Manchester South Junction and Altrincham Railway. *2010.* G. Leach

approaches to the three main stations at Leeds, all close together, formed by three goods stations and yards, two engine sheds and the split-level Holbeck passenger station.

Suburbs

Although vacant land around stations attracted new building, as occurred at Bedford and Watford for example, railways generally were not often directly responsible for suburban development. Indeed, in some instances they hindered it. Rather, their influence was indirect, largely by encouraging the growth of outlying villages possessing a station, creating infilling until they became part of the town. Much of it began in the 1860s and '70s as middle-class city workers began moving out to more congenial residential surroundings. Here the railways played their part by building stations to serve new suburbs that developed alongside their lines or, in some cases, by building suburban branch lines and loops specifically to serve them, a development that was particularly marked in

London, Glasgow, Birmingham and Manchester. There were exceptions, however. The London & Southampton Railway's first station serving Kingston-on-Thames in 1838 was over a mile away. In 1840 speculative house building prompted the railway to move the station ½ mile west. The developer's bankruptcy stopped building work in its early stages, but the presence of the station encouraged others to proceed and a new residential town grew, called Surbiton, although the station was not renamed until 1863 when another Kingston station was built on a new line. Surbiton, therefore, has some claim to be the first suburb to have been established because of the proximity of a railway. The claim to be the first suburban railway proper can be made by the Manchester South Junction & Altrincham Railway of 1849. Although not originally intended as such, it rapidly became so as suburbs grew alongside it in south Manchester and north Cheshire. It was electrified in 1931 and from 1993 became part of Manchester's Metrolink Light Rapid Transit system.

Electric trams and then buses greatly affected certain suburban railways. The Harborne branch in Birmingham of 1875 lost its passenger services in 1934 and the Nottingham

Norbury station serves a south London suburb.

From an old postcard

Suburban Railway of 1889 in 1931. Regular passenger trains on Edinburgh's Suburban & Southside Junction Railway of 1884 lingered on until 1962, but the line survived as a useful through route avoiding busy lines through the city, as did the Birmingham West Suburban Railway of 1876 that eleven years later became a part of the Midland Railway's main line from Birmingham to Bristol. In 1902 the Manchester South District Railway of 1880 similarly became the Midland's main route into the city from London. Two cities developed circular suburban routes that materially assisted growth and continue to thrive as electrified lines. South of the Clyde in Glasgow, the first section of the Cathcart District Railway was opened in 1886 and subsequently was extended to form, with other lines, the present-day Cathcart Circle. In Newcastle a series of lines formed a circular route from Central station northward through Gosforth, Whitley Bay and North Shields, aiding the growth of satellite towns that became part of the north Tyneside conurbation. One purpose-built suburban railway that was a flop managed to survive to see better days. The Great Eastern's

Maxwell Park station on Glasgow's Cathcart Circle line. *2005*.

Railway Heritage

Fairlop Loop of 1903 in metropolitan Essex did no better than its Nottingham counterpart in attracting the anticipated suburban development, but remained long enough to eventually serve new housing estates built in the 1930s and after the Second World War, finally becoming an extension of the London Underground's Central Line.

Electrification was the saviour of many suburban railways, beginning in 1903 with the conversion of the Mersey Railway serving Liverpool and Birkenhead, followed by other lines in Merseyside, Manchester, north Tyneside and, especially, London where the expanding Underground system and progressive electrification of southern suburban lines aided development well into the twentieth century. Although railway companies were statutorily barred from acquiring land for purposes other than a railway, the Metropolitan Railway managed to circumvent the legislation and between 1880 and 1930, latterly through a subsidiary company, acquired vast acreages of land for residential development along its lines extending out through Middlesex, Bucks and Herts. It adopted the slogan 'Metroland,' immortalised by John Betjeman, as in the lines:

> *Funereal from Harrow draws the train,*
> *On, on, northwestwards, London far away,*
> *And stations start to look quite countrified,*
> *Pinner, a parish of a thousand souls,*
> *Til the railways gave it many thousands more.*

In summary, it can be said that most suburban railways influenced townscapes by aiding development before succumbing to tram and bus competition, while those that were electrified have continued to do so. But much housing development in the nineteenth and early twentieth centuries was highly selective, doing little to alleviate overcrowding in city centre working-class districts. At times, the presence of a railway had the opposite effect, preventing a town's expansion by acting as a barrier. For example, the London & Greenwich Railway effectively isolated a large part of Southwark from Bermondsey. Viaducts at Wolverhampton prevented expansion eastward and northward, while for many years London Road Viaduct at Brighton inhibited northward growth. In the 1850s Coventry began to expand from a crowded, closely-knit city, mainly northward and eastward apart from a small development to the south that was virtually cut off by two railways. It was not until 1897 that bridges were built under them, enabling a new road to be constructed, whereupon the large suburb of Earlsdon rapidly took shape. At Northwich in Cheshire, the railway viaduct for many years acted as a barrier to southward expansion of the town.

In Carlisle severance was near complete. For thirty years access from the city to the growing industrial districts of Dentonholme and Newtown to the west was barred by ½ mile of the London–Glasgow main line, pierced only by two low, narrow bridges and a narrow tunnel under the station, until the city built Victoria Viaduct in 1877 to carry a broad new highway over the railway. Cambridge was similarly isolated from new industrial suburbs to the east, while at York expansion of the city westward was prevented by a large railway conurbation of junctions, yards and workshops. Railway lines and junctions on the east side of Edinburgh left only a small gap between Portobello and the rest of the city. The historic part of the small town of Cullen, in north-east Scotland, was isolated from the new town by an embankment and viaducts, only slightly mitigated by an ornamental bridge. There, however, the railway was not to blame; the Earl of Seafield refused to let it use a less obtrusive route through his grounds. At Uckfield in Sussex, an urban area called New Town grew near the station, quite separate from the historic town, with the railway acting as the divider.

Railway cuttings in towns were less divisive than viaducts and embankments. It was easier and cheaper to build bridges over rather than under. In 1840 the small town of Belper in Derbyshire, for instance, was cut through by the North Midland Railway in a narrow, stone-lined cutting – which reduced the land-take – given a degree of elegance by curved walls. Severance was mitigated by ten overbridges within a mile. The railway through Gravesend also was largely hidden in the same manner.

Chapter 5

PLACES THE RAILWAYS MADE

The effect of railway houses on the countryside, singly or in small groups, has already been touched on in chapter 2. Wherever there was a concentration of railway activity, whether a station, junction, marshalling yard, an engine shed, workshops or any combination of them, houses for the workforce were needed in much larger numbers. Some were provided by private builders, but many were built by the railways themselves in uniform streets or terraces, either in an existing town, where often they formed a distinctive railway suburb or quarter, or as an entirely new town or village. They made a readily identifiable contribution to both townscapes and the rural scene that was rarely other than detrimental, although in this respect railways were no worse than most other heavy industries and better than some. They were not alone in creating company communities, of course. From the early years of the Industrial Revolution, mill and mine owners had built houses and villages for their workers. The railways simply did it on a far larger scale, to the extent that by 1920, collectively they were the largest single housing landlord in the country, owning some 27,000 dwellings occupied by employees.

Railway towns

The first railway town built from scratch was begun by the Stockton & Darlington Railway to serve its new workshops at the hamlet of Shildon in County Durham. By the early 1830s the town housed a population of 900, many in company houses. By 1902, with the addition of private houses, it had grown to close on 2,500, and by the 1970s over 15,000, almost entirely due to progressive enlargement of the works. The second was also at a small village, Wolverton in Buckinghamshire, where in 1838 the London & Birmingham Railway established workshops conveniently located halfway between its termini and on a canal for the delivery of materials. Unlike the unplanned growth of Shildon, a regular pattern of streets was laid out containing terraces of uniform houses, a church, market hall and schools for a population that grew from some 350 to over 7,000 in 1902 – over half of which were railway employees – and some 13,000 in 1931. Apart from a printing works, Wolverton was still essentially a railway town and had spilled over into the neighbouring parish of Bradwell where three streets of 202 houses had been built, called New Bradwell.

In the early 1840s Britain's two best known railway towns followed contemporaneously: Crewe and Swindon. Crewe was the only one that was built entirely in open countryside. It was laid out in mid-Cheshire in an orderly fashion by the engineer Joseph Locke and the architect John Cunningham for the Grand Junction Railway, whose works at Edge Hill, Liverpool, were outgrown. The new town was complete with a school, assembly room, a courthouse and church, and received its first residents in 1843, when a mass influx of 800 employees and their families arrived from Edge Hill. Five years later there were 520 houses built by the London & North Western Railway, of which the Grand Junction was now part, together with 300 privately built. Eventually the railway owned over 900 houses and had provided more schools, a hospital, four churches, baths and a park. In 1911 the population was 45,000

Early London & North Western Railway houses in Betley Street, Crewe. *1992.*

and Crewe remained purely a railway town until new industries arrived in the 1930s.

Swindon, on the other hand, was built close to an existing small Wiltshire market town, where the Great Western Railway bought land for a works and a new town in 1841. Like Crewe, it was well laid out, to the design of I.K. Brunel assisted by the architect Francis Thompson, and ten years later had a population of 4,800, a church, school, library, market hall and mechanics' institute. For the next fifty years New Swindon slowly grew until it joined the old town, physically and socially, and in 1900 they were incorporated as a single borough. In the 1930s the combined population approached 63,000, new industries were being attracted and Swindon was no longer solely a railway town.

As a railway town Barrow-in-Furness was unique. It began as a handful of houses at a pier used for exporting iron ore and slate brought by road from local mines and quarries. In 1846 the Furness Railway was opened for the same purpose, expanding but remaining isolated from the main network until 1857. Meanwhile, the railway company embarked on building a new town, laying out wide streets with a church, town hall, market,

The first estate of Great Western houses at Swindon. *1993.*

Blocks of Furness
Railway tenements
in Island Road,
Barrow-in-Furness.
1993.

gas and waterworks, schools and, most importantly, docks. At
the same time it invested in iron and steelworks, a jute factory
and a shipyard. Barrow was a boom town, its population rising
from 3,000 in 1861 to six times that number in the 1870s. The
steelworks, in which the railway had a substantial stake, was
the largest in Britain, and its acreage of docks, wholly railway-
owned, was exceeded only by London and Liverpool. Barrow
and the Furness Railway were as synonymous as Crewe was
with the London & North Western and Swindon with the GWR.
But Barrow did not last. The decline of iron ore deposits
reduced maritime traffic and outside interests steadily took over
the town's other industries. Population growth tailed off and
by the end of the century Barrow was primarily a shipbuilding
town with a steelworks. The railway was still hugely influential,
but no longer the dominant force.

Somewhat earlier, similar mushroom-like growth created
Middlesbrough, but on a larger scale. In 1830 the pioneer Stockton
& Darlington Railway extended its line from Stockton-on-Tees to
a new deep-water port nearer the mouth of the river, built on open

land by a group of the railway's promoters. They named it Middlesbrough and laid out a small town on a grid pattern. By 1841 there were 5,700 inhabitants and, like Barrow, it attracted iron and steelworks. In 1881 the population was 56,000. By 1911 it had almost doubled, by which time Middlesbrough had become the country's largest centre of the iron and steel industry. Strong connections were maintained with the railway, which in 1849 had bought the dock. By 1874 its successor, the North Eastern company, had enlarged it to over twice the original size.

Nineteenth-century South Wales was a much larger boom area. Its high quality coal was in demand worldwide, and to export it local railways and existing small ports underwent rapid expansion. An exception was Barry which, like Barrow and Middlesbrough, was built on virgin land, this time by a combined undertaking, the Barry Dock & Railway Company. Late on the scene, it was established in 1884 to break the coal exporting monopoly of the Taff Vale Railway and the Bute dock interests at Cardiff. From what *The Builder* in 1891 commented had been 'a barren beach with a farmhouse and two or three scattered cottages' with a population of eighty-five, in ten years there mushroomed docks, railways and a town of 13,000. By the time growth had passed its peak in 1931 there were 39,000 inhabitants. Although the dock and railway company itself did not lay out the town, it strongly influenced its pattern and development. Without the company Barry would not have come into being and in that sense, therefore, it was a railway town, albeit of a different kind.

Horwich in 1884 was little more than a Lancashire village with a small cotton mill and bleach works. That year the Lancashire & Yorkshire Railway moved in with a new locomotive works, but relied on local builders to erect houses for which the railway provided land, together with a mechanics' institute and a few other amenities. By 1891 the railway had tripled the population and eventually employed 4,000 workers, yet played little part in the physical development of Horwich as a railway town, leaving its layout and housing primarily to private interests.

Much the same happened at Eastleigh, Hampshire, but in a less orderly manner to the extent that a public enquiry was held into the bad housing. It was provided by speculative builders when the London & South Western Railway moved its carriage and wagon works from London in 1891, followed by locomotive building in 1903-10. Originating as a small village called Bishopstoke, the population quickly rose from 600 to 3,500 and by 1911 had reached 15,200, but other than providing a mechanics' institute the railway company played little active part in the town's development.

The smallest railway town of this kind was built on an open site in north Norfolk at Melton Constable, where a small works was opened by the Lynn & Fakenham Railway in 1882, eventually becoming the home of the Midland & Great Northern Joint Railway, under which the works expanded, together with public services, schools and a railway institute. The joint companies also built some houses, and a population of 118 in 1881 had grown to 1,157 in 1911, all railway families. It was urban in character and called itself a town, although in size it was never more than a large village, and after the railway closed in 1964 the population fell to 650. Today there is very little to indicate that it was once a railway community.

To a considerable extent these were all company towns. There were others which, although they owed their origin or growth to the railway, could not be called that. Redhill in Surrey began as a station at a junction in open country nearly 2 miles from the town of Reigate. It attracted new housing and soon outstripped its ancient neighbour, growing three times larger until they were united as a single borough. Meanwhile, the commercial centre had become established at Redhill. Similar expansion took place at other London, Brighton & South Coast Railway country stations at Hassocks, Horley and Haywards Heath, and elsewhere when the railway made commuting convenient.

When the first section of the Lancaster & Carlisle Railway opened in 1846 a station was built at Carnforth, where there were no more than some 300 inhabitants. Eleven years later it became a junction with the Furness Railway and in 1867 with the Midland as well. All three companies built engine sheds and yards, and the London & North Western, of which the Lancaster & Carlisle was now a part, and the Midland built terraces of

A row of Midland Railway houses at Carnforth, Lancashire. *2012.*

distinctive houses, although the Furness did not. Carnforth had become a railway town, but not for long. In 1864 an iron and steel works was begun. It, too, built workers' houses and by 1875-6 the population was 2,600, of which 60 per cent of the workforce were railway employees. Railway dominance was regained when the iron works closed in 1929, but was lost again when the combined locomotive depot closed in 1969. The station was reduced in size, although Carnforth is still a junction and the town has continued to grow.

Until 1844 Didcot was an old Berkshire village, now in Oxfordshire. In that year it became a junction on the Great Western Railway and a station bearing its name was opened at Northbourne, ½ mile away, together with an engine shed. When the shed was considerably enlarged in 1857 sidings were added, the small railway community gained an influx of more railway workers and it became known as Newtown, with a population of 369 in 1871. In 1884 the GWR built a large provender store for its 3,000-odd horses, a four-storey building with a tall water tower that, until it was demolished in 1976, was a prominent feature in the landscape. Steadily the two villages extended towards each other until in 1932 they had become one, with a combined population of 2,200. Most of the railwaymen's houses were built by private builders; the Great Western did not build any until 1903, and then only thirty-two. Didcot now is no longer primarily a railway settlement; post-Second World War development and diversification have made it into a small town. A similar transformation took place after 1848 when the Great Western opened a station at Westbury, a mainly Georgian village in Wiltshire. Two years later it became a junction, with a small engine shed, and in 1906 it became a much more important junction on the GWR's new main line to the west, with a larger station, engine shed and yards. Like Carnforth, Westbury also had an iron works from 1857 to 1925, helping to transform it into a small town of 4,000 by 1932 and now well over twice that number, although apart from a few houses there was no distinctive railway quarter as such.

Railway enclaves

Railway districts or enclaves in existing towns were far more numerous, consisting of groups of railwaymens' houses, company and private, alongside workshops, locomotive depots and marshalling yards. Although essentially a part of their host towns, sharing their services, they possessed their own characteristics, setting them apart, sometimes growing to be a dominant feature that turned the original town into what primarily amounted to a railway town.

Until recent times Derby probably was the best known, a county town and regional centre with several industries and, when the railway arrived in 1839-40, a population of well over 25,000. Its municipal authorities were sufficiently influential to insist on three railway companies building a joint station a mile out of town. The companies also built workshops there and, after amalgamating as the Midland Railway, set up headquarters next to the station. To a small group of company houses many more were added, privately built, the whole forming a large and distinct railway complex that adjoined but in many ways was separate from the town. After 1873 the carriage and wagon

works were moved to another site in Derby, forming a second railway enclave to the south west, where more railway houses were built. Derby now was virtually synonymous with the Midland Railway and although in the early twentieth century other industries moved in, it continued for many years to be regarded as a railway town, and in 1947, despite new industries, the LMS Railway was the second largest employer.

The railway played a major role in creating modern Doncaster, mainly due to the efforts of one man, Edmund Denison, chairman of the Great Northern Railway which, in 1852, decided to move its works from Boston to somewhere more convenient. Peterborough was a strong contender but Denison, who had local interests, and his boardroom allies prevailed and in a short time the population of the small market town increased by some 2,500. The new works was built next to the station, but the engine sheds and yards were further south, resulting in Doncaster having two major railway enclaves. The houses were mostly built privately, although the company did provide schools. Peterborough did not lose out entirely. The Great Northern had an engine shed close to the

Early North Midland Railway houses opposite Derby Station, designed by Francis Thompson in 1841. *1983.*

station and, later, a larger one, workshops and marshalling yards north of the town at New England, with a colony of some 220 houses, schools and a gas works strung out in linear fashion alongside the railway. The Great Eastern, Midland and London & North Western railways also had locomotive sheds at Peterborough, the first two with repair shops as well, so railways were very prominent in the townscape and were by far the largest employer.

Until 1910 the North Eastern Railway's works were at Gateshead, but with no distinct railway community. Then the works was transferred to Darlington, greatly expanding a smaller works dating from Stockton & Darlington days, along with a palatial new office building for the mechanical engineering department. In 1923 a new wagon works was added. All three were in separate locations, but as the town was already a centre of heavy engineering the railway was not as dominant as at other railway towns and, apart from some limited company housing, a railway quarter did not emerge in the same manner. Neither did one at Brighton, where the London, Brighton & South Coast Railway established its works in 1852, being the sole industry of any consequence. In 1903 the railway employed over 2,000 and several small groups of houses were built, the largest, of 125, at Preston Park, but otherwise there was no recognisable railway quarter. Although, as Jack Simmons has remarked in *The Railway in Town and Country*, the railway transformed Brighton, it was not so much by its physical presence but by its fast and frequent train service from London, making it easy to reach for a day out, a weekend, a holiday or, for the London businessman, a daily commute.

Rather different kinds of railway communities grew at three towns, where railway companies and private builders' locomotive works were close together. The largest was at Springburn in Glasgow, where they were important contributors to the city's world-wide reputation for heavy engineering. In 1903 three firms amalgamated into the North British Locomotive Company. Henry Dübs & Co's Queens Park works was at Polmadie next to the Caledonian Railway's principal engine sheds on the south side of the city. The Atlas and Hyde Park works of Sharp Stewart & Co and Neilson Reid & Co respectively were at Springburn to the north, where the North British and Caledonian Railways also had their works, Cowlairs and St Rollox, together making Springburn the largest concentration of locomotive building anywhere, employing three out of every four in the whole industry. The Edinburgh & Glasgow Railway, predecessor to the North British, began in 1864 to build a model village at Springburn for its workers, designed by the Perth architect Andrew Heiton. It was to comprise a series of tenement blocks around a central square containing shops and an ornamental fountain, a school, library and recreation ground, but only four terraces were completed before the cost was considered too great. Built on a hillside, they were a well-known landmark until they were demolished in 1967.

A similar but smaller railway suburb developed at Gorton in east Manchester, where in 1846 the Manchester, Sheffield & Lincolnshire Railway (later the Great Central) established its works, together with 140 houses, a school, library and institute. In 1854 the well-known locomotive builders Beyer Peacock built a large works close by.

In 1855 the Glasgow & South Western Railway moved its works from Glasgow to Kilmarnock in Ayrshire. The railway engineering works of Andrew Barclay had been there since 1840, and in 1859 they, too, began locomotive building, followed by Dick, Kerr & Co. All three works were close together, forming a railway colony west of the station. The Glasgow & South Western built a small estate of houses east of the town near its large engine shed at Hurlford. In 1897 the same company began a much larger model village at Corkerhill, south of the Clyde in Glasgow, next to its new engine sheds. Eventually there were 132 dwellings in ten two-storey tenement blocks, forming a self-contained community where the company provided all services, a large institute that also served as a church, a library, reading room, baths and a large general store. The earlier tenements had some architectural pretensions, with crow-stepped gables. All have now been demolished. In the same period the Caledonian built some quite distinguished superior tenements and shops, as investment properties next to several of their new Glasgow urban stations at Kelvinbridge, Anderston Cross and Glasgow Cross, and the North British at Bridgeton Cross, all designed by well-known architects.

Railway tenement blocks for employees were built in London: one at King's Cross, four at St Pancras and at Vauxhall, eight in Bermondsey. Colonies of company houses at concentrations of engine sheds, workshops and yards grew at Cricklewood, Willesden, Neasden – where there were two, on opposite sides of the line – New Cross and Slade Green. London's largest railway quarter was at Stratford, where the Eastern Counties Railway built its works in 1848. They were progressively enlarged by the Great Eastern together with junctions and yards, and included 300 houses called New Town.

Some small towns where there was extensive railway development still managed to retain their identity. Ashford, in Kent, for example,

Ashford Works gatehouse, South Eastern Railway. *2001.* G. Beecroft

was a market town of some 3,700 inhabitants when, in 1845, the South Eastern Railway moved its works from London. Samuel Beazley, a good architect, laid out an estate just outside, with a chapel, school and institute centred on a green. It remained separate from its parent and later attracted other industries. By 1911 the combined population was close on 17,000. In much the same way the historic Lancashire borough of Newton-le-Willows became host to Earlestown, a railway colony of some 340 unappealing standard London & North Western company houses next to its wagon works. It was preceded by a private locomotive builder, the Vulcan Foundry, established on a rural site in 1833 alongside the Warrington & Newton Railway, with its own small group of houses called Vulcan Village. But although administratively Earlestown became part of Newton, it stayed largely separate. A similar but smaller development took place in Scotland where, in 1901-5, the Great North of Scotland Railway moved its locomotive works from Kittybrewster, where there was already a railway colony just north of Aberdeen, to a larger site at the small town of Inverurie, where the company built a well laid-out estate of two-storey

Part of the Great North of Scotland Railway estate at Inverurie. *1990.*

tenement houses for its 500 employees, with a public park and allotment gardens.

Oswestry, in Shropshire close to the Welsh border, was home to the Cambrian Railways' headquarters and works. Despite a doubling of the population between 1861 and 1911, there was no distinguishable railway enclave as such, apart from the works itself on the edge of the town. It was much the same at March, a small medieval Cambridgeshire village, where engine sheds and extensive marshalling yards were laid out by the Great Eastern Railway in 1889 and its successor, the London & North Eastern, in 1933. The local population grew by more than a quarter, yet only forty-one company houses were built.

Lastly, three old and well-established towns that also became regarded as railway towns after becoming important junctions with a large station, engine sheds and marshalling yards. The first two, York and Carlisle, were historic cities and regional centres where, as we have seen in chapter 4, the railway also acted as a divider, separating them into two parts. Six lines met at York, eventually coming under the control of one large company, the North Eastern, which established locomotive, carriage and wagon works there. Latterly they were devoted solely to carriage building. More importantly, York was chosen for the headquarters offices, in which sense the city ranked with Derby as a railway town monopolised by a single large company. It also possesses one of Britain's finest stations.

The opposite happened at Carlisle, where eight lines of seven different railways met, converging on one large station. Each company had its own locomotive depot, yards, goods station and colony of houses, forming a patchwork of railway enclaves. But unlike York, Carlisle already had other well-established industries and the railway, although important, was not dominant.

Thirdly, a smaller town that became well known as an important railway junction with a large station: Rugby, in Warwickshire, where six lines of the London & North Western Railway converged, together with one of the Midland. In 1866 it was immortalised as 'Mugby Junction' in Charles Dickens' *All the Year Round*. Rugby was a small market town best known for its public school. The railway passed about ½ mile to the north, creating a broad 1½ mile long swathe of junctions, sidings, station, workshops and engine sheds, forming a boundary with open country and crossed by roads at only three points. Steadily the gap between town and railway was filled with streets and houses, but it was not until the turn of the nineteenth century that the barrier was broken when a large electrical engineering works was built on the other side of the tracks, ending the railway's monopoly as Rugby's main employer. In 1899 a third railway, the Great Central, passed along the east side of the town, but made no junction. Yet considering the railways' dominance for over half a century, it seems strange that, despite employing a total of 1,350, none of the companies built houses, apart from a small square erected in the early years by the London & Birmingham Railway and now demolished.

Railway villages

Clusters of railway houses were often found next to country junctions, either as an adjunct to an existing village or as a new community in open country, sometimes at quite isolated locations, changing the local landscape in the process. One of the earliest was established by the Stanhope & Tyne Railroad at the head of a cable-worked incline at Waskerley, a remote spot high on the moors of County Durham. By 1849, when it had become part of the Stockton & Darlington Railway, there were two engine sheds, a wagon repair shop and store, some thirty houses, a post office, school, two chapels and an institute. When the line closed in 1968, apart from a few buildings the village had already been abandoned for some fifteen years. Now it is not easy to imagine there was ever a railway there. In the Scottish Borders on the North British Railway's Waverley Route from Edinburgh to Carlisle, Riccarton Junction was even more remote. Existing solely as a station for changing trains, it was 2 miles from a public road, and its railway community of thirty-odd houses, school and recreation hall clustered next to it was totally reliant on the railway for all services.

There were several other junctions that were merely exchange stations with neither road access nor a community beyond one or two houses. Roudham Junction in Norfolk and Killin Junction in western Scotland were two. There was a clutch in mid-Wales: Moat Lane Junction, Dovey Junction and Barmouth Junction, now renamed Morfa Mawddach. The last was on a road, as were two more further south, Three Cocks (named after an inn) and Talyllyn junctions, but none of them had a village. Moat Lane was the largest in the group, with a small engine shed and a staff of around sixty, most of whom seem to have lived at Caersws, a mile away. Georgemas Junction in the far north of Scotland, similarly remote, also had road access and in 2014 gained greater prominence when a road-rail transshipment yard was opened for nuclear flasks from the plant at Dounreay.

For some years Battersby Junction in North Yorkshire was roadless until one was made to connect it to Battersby village a mile away. Where public access existed a few houses might spring up, eventually forming a small village that took the railway name, such as Seaton Junction and Sidmouth Junction in south Devon. Although the stations have long been closed, 'Junction' is still part of the postal address, while at Halwill Junction in north Devon and Udny Station in Aberdeenshire the railway itself has gone. The names are now the only indications that there was once a railway there. Similarly Verney Junction in Buckinghamshire no longer has a working railway. Originally there was only a hotel and a crossing house, and even today there is merely a handful of additional houses, yet it retains its name and is well-signed from as far away as 1¼ miles. Although the line is now being restored as part of a new east-west cross-country electrified route, there will still be no junction at Verney. Two settlements in County Durham grew around stations, taking their names. Ferryhill Station is separate from Ferryhill itself, but was named after the station opened in 1844. Fifty years later it contained several rows of houses and two auction marts. In the south of the county

Despite Verney Junction having closed in 1968, leaving only a handful of houses and a hotel, the Buckinghamshire hamlet is still prominently signed. *2015.* A.J. Aitken

Station Town grew around Wingate station, opened in 1846, and in the same period grew to fourteen terraces in six streets. Again, the stations themselves are now closed.

The 14 miles of the Lancaster & Carlisle Railway where it passes through the eastern edge of the Lake District, provides good examples of three different kinds of railway village. In 1846, the year the line opened, a branch was made to Kendal. A small station and engine shed at the junction, in open country near Kendal, was named Oxenholme after a nearby farm. In 1880-82, after the London & North Western had taken over, the station and shed were enlarged, followed by two groups of LNWR houses in stern red brick terraces, ¼ mile apart, one for the station staff and the other for the locomotive department, completely inimical to their surroundings. A reading room, mission and allotments were provided. After the 1914-18 war the gap between the two groups was gradually closed by private housing.

Further north, in 1861, a branch to Ingleton was opened from Low Gill, where there was just a farm, a handful of scattered

The two railways that met at Tebay, on the West Coast main line, each built numbers of houses forming a separate railway village. Here is a North Eastern Railway terrace in Church Street. *1997*.

houses and a tiny station situated where the line entered the Lune gorge. A larger station was built at the junction, together with ten stone-built railway cottages and a school in an attractive traditional style that blended well into the landscape, forming a compact community. In the same year a third junction was made 4 miles further on near the village of Tebay, where the South Durham & Lancashire Union Railway, later part of the North Eastern system, came in from the east. As has been mentioned earlier, both railways established separate engine sheds. A railway village grew, much larger than the other two, comprising houses built by both companies. Four terraces, two for each company, totalling fifty-six houses, stand starkly on the bare hillside overlooking the railway, two in LNWR red brick and two by the NER in stone. A further fourteen less prominent NER houses stand close to a church that was jointly financed by the railways. A market hall, institute, assembly rooms, a chapel and more houses made the railway village much larger than its parent ¼ mile away, which was renamed Old Tebay.

On the Settle & Carlisle line the Midland Railway built twenty-two recognisable company houses close to the station at the isolated Hawes Junction, later renamed Garsdale although there is no village as such. Apart from a Methodist chapel, the only facilities were those provided by the railway. A similar railway village was built at Craven Arms, a Shropshire junction on the Shrewsbury & Hereford line and named after an isolated inn. There the railway colony acted as a catalyst for substantial development that by 1904 had become a sizeable village in its own right, with a gas works and cattle market. Llandudno Junction in North Wales owes its origin to a small group of railway houses next to the station opened in 1858. By 1900 it was a large village and is a now a small town, quite separate from the resort of Llandudno 3 miles away. Yet at Builth Road in mid-Wales, where lines of the Cambrian and the London & North Western intersected, each with its own station and the latter with a small engine shed, there was never anything more than the three terraces of LNWR houses put down in open country. In 1906 the Fishguard & Rosslare Railways & Harbours Company, of which the Great Western was joint owner, opened a new port

at Fishguard, and for its employees built an estate of over 100 houses called Harbour Village on a cliff top at Goodwick, overlooking the harbour.

These are all examples of railway villages pure and simple. Railway settlements as appendages to existing villages were more numerous. Small ones were easily absorbed into a village, but some remained separate. Among the latter, Hellifield in North Yorkshire retains two small colonies of former railway houses quite separate from the village, one built by the Midland Railway near the station and its engine shed, and the other by the Lancashire & Yorkshire Railway which had its own shed close to the junction of the two lines. Similarly at Barnetby in Lincolnshire the railway colony was apart from the village. At Saltney, just inside Wales near Chester, the London & North Western Railway built over 100 houses, a block of enginemen's lodgings, schools, an institute and shops, to serve the large Mold Junction engine shed alongside Saltney Ferry Station,

Wye View, part of the London & North Western Railway's village built in open country next to Builth Road station on the Mid Wales line. *1989.*

completely overshadowing the original small hamlet. Carstairs Junction in Lanarkshire took its name from a village a mile or so away, growing into an extensive railway settlement largely owned by the Caledonian Railway and eventually becoming an ecclesiastical parish in its own right, but remaining separate from the original Carstairs, which it still is.

In 1846 the ambitiously-named Manchester, Buxton, Matlock & Midlands Junction Railway was authorised to build a railway from the Derby–Sheffield line at Ambergate up the Derwent valley in Derbyshire, but by 1849 it had given up when it had only reached Rowsley, a small village of 500 people near Chatsworth. There it stopped until the Midland Railway took over in 1860 and resumed building to Buxton, eventually reaching Manchester. A marshalling yard and large engine shed were opened at Rowsley and a succession of railway houses gradually enveloped the old village until, by the 1890s, it was predominantly a railway settlement. At the end of the century something similar happened when the adjacent Northamptonshire villages of Woodford Halse and Hinton found themselves on the new Great Central Railway, which

The London & North Western Railway built a large settlement at Mold Junction near Chester, comprising houses, a school and enginemen's lodging house. *1991.*

passed between them. The place became an important junction with an engine shed, wagon workshop and marshalling yard. In this case the 170 houses for railway workers were built by private developers and leased to the railway company, along with shops and a gas works. Woodford and Hinton had become predominantly a railway village.

Several railway villages of a different kind were established in Scotland in the early nineteenth century, not by railway companies but strongly influenced by their presence, part of a movement by large landowners to build planned villages for housing their workers in the era of agricultural improvement. In Strathmore, north of Dundee, two were begun in the 1830s, one at Newtyle, for a time the terminus of the Dundee & Newtyle Railway, and another at Ardler, originally named

Midland Railway houses at Rowsley, Derbyshire. *1992.*

Washington, on the Dundee & Coupar Angus Railway. Like most of the planned villages they were rectilinear in layout, at Ardler straddling the railway, which crossed streets on the level, a matter of little consequence at a time when it was horse operated. The line was diverted in the 1840s when it became part of the Scottish Midland Junction Railway, later on the main route from Glasgow to Aberdeen. Ladybank in Fife began as a small planned village that grew when the railway came, and eventually became a burgh.

In the 1850s the Edinburgh & Glasgow Railway exercised a more direct influence in creating the village of Lenzie when it offered several years' free season tickets to occupiers of new houses built on virgin sites near the railway. It was an attempt to create commuter traffic, and resulted in a new development close to the isolated station of Campsie Junction. The new community named itself Lenzie, in 1867 the station name was changed, and by 1891 there was a population of 1,600. In 1897 the Highland Railway made land available for housing and shops at Kyle of Lochalsh in an attempt to stimulate growth at the end of their new line serving Skye. It was part of a similar effort by a number of railways, including the East Lancashire Railway some forty years earlier which offered free first-class season tickets to Liverpool from Aintree, Maghull, Town Green, Ormskirk and Burscough to commuters buying houses having more than £50 annual value, varying in validity from seven to eighteen years according to their distance from the city, thereby contributing to the growth of the satellite towns. Towards the century's end the London & North Western offered what it called house passes from selected stations between Euston and Watford such as Harrow, and from Alderley Edge to Manchester, again stimulating growth. As we have seen, several railways tried to develop seaside resorts with a similar incentive, but with little real success. In all these instances, as with the Metropolitan Railway's creation of 'Metroland' in the early 1900s, the railways not only gained passenger traffic but carried materials for new roads and houses. In the inter-war years the London Underground built new extensions and the Southern Railway new stations, both deliberately preceding housing development,

although the latter's new branch line to Allhallows-on-Sea in 1932 was a failure and closed in 1961.

Another different kind of railway village was the temporary settlement of rudimentary wooden huts built by railway contractors at sites where their workers and their families could not be accommodated in the local community. Best known is the series on the remote Pennine moorlands traversed by the Settle & Carlisle line, built in 1870-76. The largest, Batty Green at Ribblehead, housed over 2,000 and was provided with a school, mission room, library and hospital. Today, only grassy mounds and hollows indicate their sites. A permanent village of thirty cottages was built by the North Midland Railway in 1838 to house workers building Clay Cross Tunnel in Derbyshire, now all demolished. A larger settlement still stands at Sudbrook on

Houses built at Sudbrook for workers building the Severn Tunnel. The large tunnel pumping station is at the end of the street. *2014.*

the Welsh side of the Severn estuary, built in 1880-89 by the Severn Tunnel contractor T.A. Walker. Nine brick and stone terraces still stand, together with one built of concrete blocks – a particularly early example of this construction – some managers' houses, a former school, post office and hospital. Nearby is an imposing engine house and other buildings that contained steam boilers, pumps and ventilation fans for the tunnel. In the mid-1880s William Arrol built two colonies for his Forth Bridge contract. The larger one, at North Queensferry, like Ribblehead comprised streets of temporary huts. At Dalmeny on the south bank, however, brick houses for senior staff still stand, although the sixty tenements which accompanied them have gone.

Chapter 6

Chapter 6

ABANDONED RAILWAYS

Almost every Ordnance Survey map, except those covering remote parts of Scotland, will show broken lines marked 'Dismtd rly', running across the countryside through cuttings, along embankments and across viaducts. They are familiar features in the landscape which we tend to associate with the mass closures of railways in the 1960s, the so-called 'Beeching era', although in fact they were not new. Well over 500 sites date from the nineteenth century and a significant number from the late eighteenth or earlier, the latter being remains of horse-drawn tramroads or wagonways.

One of the oldest with discernible remains is the former cable-worked incline that took coal from the Parker Pit down to the harbour at Whitehaven in west Cumbria, dating from 1738. Most of these somewhat primitive early railways carried coal or stone from mines and quarries to the nearest navigable river, canal or harbour, and some forty sites are listed or are scheduled Ancient Monuments. Remains can be found from Cornwall to Fife and are especially numerous in South Wales, comprising earthworks, inclines, bridges, a few tunnels and some viaducts, mostly

Remains of the Haytor Granite Tramroad on Dartmoor, which had stone blocks for rails. *1984.*

The world's oldest viaduct, Laigh Milton on the Kilmarnock & Troon Railway of 1812, in 1987 before restoration.

modest structures although Bont Fawr Viaduct at Pontryhdyfen in West Glamorgan has four 70ft arches an impressive 75ft high. An Ancient Monument, it dates from 1824-27 and also carries a water channel that supplied a wheel at Oakwood Ironworks. At Merthyr Tydfil the Pantycafnan Bridge of 1793 can claim to be the first iron railway bridge. It too carried a water channel and is a scheduled Ancient Monument.

Nineteenth-century abandonments left more prominent landmarks and are far more numerous, so a selection will have to suffice. The boom years of the Railway Manias of the 1840s and 1860s produced projects that were started but not completed. The 200yds of cutting in a field at Hurst Green, near Clitheroe in the Ribble Valley of north Lancashire, is all that remains of the grandly-titled Fleetwood, Preston & West Riding Junction Railway of the 1840s, raising the question why digging was begun on this short isolated section. The Oxford & Rugby Railway of 1849 stopped in a field when it

A disused rock cutting on the 1840 Glyncorrwg Mineral Railway near Tonna in South Wales. *2005.*

reached Knightcote in Warwickshire, overtaken by its purchase by the GWR-backed Oxford & Birmingham Railway that continued the line on a more direct route, leaving a few hundred yards of embankment pointing in the direction of Rugby. The 1860s brought similar failures, such as the 2 miles of abandoned earthworks in Sussex between Balcombe and Uckfield, evidence of an ambitious scheme to shorten the London, Brighton & South Coast Railway's route to Hastings. The Furness Railway's even more ambitious scheme to shorten its route up the Cumbrian coast from Barrow by building a viaduct across the Duddon estuary was also abandoned after completing a few earthworks near Askam.

More substantial remains mark railways that were completed but never brought into use, often the result of intense but abortive inter-company rivalry, such as the short curve at Bruton in Somerset, built in the 1860s to connect the Somerset Central Railway with the Bristol & Exeter, and the impressive 11-arch Wharfe Viaduct at Tadcaster, North Yorkshire, of 1847-49, intended to shorten the route from Leeds to York. The Manchester & Milford Railway was an even more grandiose failure. By building a 50 mile link between existing railways in the middle of Wales, a shorter route would be gained from industrial northwest England to a new Atlantic port on Milford Haven.

A derelict cutting on the over-ambitious Manchester & Milford Railway at Llangurig. It never saw a train. *2015*.

Bordesley Viaduct carries the Great Western line into Birmingham. Beyond it can be seen Duddeston Viaduct, intended to link it with the London & North Western's line, but never used.

Hopelessly impracticable, nevertheless by 1864 it had managed to build 3 miles of line between Llanidloes and Llangurig, complete with track and signalling. Only a few contractors' and goods trains ever used it, and in 1882 the track was removed, leaving substantial earthworks and bridges. Today its connecting lines also have been closed, leaving their own landmarks. A 3 mile line was built in 1873 between Stoke Golding and Hinckley in Leicestershire, intended to avoid busy junctions at Nuneaton. It is not known whether it ever carried trains, but it only lasted until 1889 before being taken up. The most outstanding monument to fruitless Victorian railway rivalry is the Duddeston Viaduct in Birmingham, referred to in chapter 5; never used except as a siding. As recently as 1922-23 the Great Western built the infrastructure for a new line in the Clydach Valley of West Glamorgan, including stations, but failed to lay any track in the central section, leaving two dead-end branches. In the late 1930s the same company began a new line to Looe in Cornwall, part of an ambitious scheme to create a new resort, but the Second World War stopped work. After assuming control of the South Wales railways at the 1923 Grouping, the GWR attempted to rationalise several competing parallel lines, including closure of 2¾ miles of the former Barry Railway near Caerphilly which was duplicated by the Rhymney Railway, leaving two large trestle viaducts standing disused for over twenty years.

The closure of working lines occurred as early as 1851 with the abandonment of 12 miles of the Newmarket Railway between Great Chesterford and Six Mile Bottom in Cambridgeshire, in favour of an alternative route. Remains can still be seen. On the Oxford–Cambridge line, connecting curves to other lines were built at Wolvercot and Bletchley, closed in 1861 and 1864 respectively. The Bletchley south curve was re-opened in 1934 and closed again in the 1960s. Both have left substantial embankments. South of Tuxford in Nottinghamshire, in 1891-92 the Great Northern Railway main line was crossed by the ambitiously-named Lancashire, Derbyshire and East Coast Railway (it reached neither Lancashire nor the east coast) at Dukeries Junction. West-to-north and south connecting curves were made, but on the latter no rails were ever laid until 2012 when the old embankment was used for a test track. In 1862 the Eden Valley line in Cumbria made a curious south-facing junction with the West Coast main line at Clifton, south of Penrith, but after only fourteen months it became disused on being superseded by a more sensible north-facing curve, although it was not officially closed until 1875, leaving a visible trackbed, partly in a cutting with two road over-bridges. Now it has been filled in and absorbed into adjacent land, only the parapets of one of the bridges standing in-congruously in a field. Under its Act of 1863, the Midland Railway built a 1¼ mile line from the London & North Western's St Albans branch at Park Street to carry construction trains to Napsbury on the new line it was building to London. After completion the connection was abandoned, although it is still very visible. Similarly, a short contractors' curve was made on the London & South Western main line to

This bridge in a field at Clifton, near Penrith, is a reminder of a short-lived railway that closed as long ago as 1862. *2015.*

assist in construction of the Somerset Central Railway which crossed it at Templecombe. In 1877 the Midland opened a branch to Hemel Hempstead from its London line at Harpenden, Hertfordshire. The junction faced north, but in 1888 it was changed to a much more convenient one facing south, abandoning the original curve which can still be seen from a passing train. Remains of lines to ferries made redundant by the Severn Tunnel and the Forth Bridge are still in evidence, while a much longer redundant railway is well visible at several places between Saltash and St Germans in Cornwall. There, in 1908, some 5 miles of Brunel's original route were replaced by a new one to avoid the expense of rebuilding five of his timber viaducts. Even so, the replacement line still needed two viaducts and a tunnel.

The large-scale closures by British Railways in the 1960s left whole areas of Britain with trackless railways. North Devon, north Norfolk and Speyside are examples. Industrial and urban districts also lost secondary routes and branch lines, many of them now built over. Some particularly long sections of secondary routes were abandoned in the process, most notably the 98 miles of the Waverley Route from Edinburgh to Carlisle; 56 miles on the mid-Wales line of the former Cambrian Railways, together with a further 50-odd miles over its southward continuation, the Brecon & Merthyr Railway, to Newport; the 71-mile Somerset & Dorset line from Bath to Bournemouth; the Stainmore line across the northern Pennines from Bishop Auckland to Tebay, 72 miles; and a group of connected lines totalling 78 miles in Perthshire, bordered by Dunblane, Gleneagles, Perth and Crianlarich. The most notable main line loss was the whole of the Great Central Railway from Nottinghamshire to Buckinghamshire, 73 miles, of which well over half has since disappeared through redevelopment. Sixteen miles of the former Midland main line through the Peak District are readily distinguished by viaducts and tunnels. In Scotland most of the former Caledonian Railway main line from Perth to Aberdeen was closed in favour of an alternative but longer route via Dundee, leaving 45 miles of trackbed through Strathmore. As recently as 1983, 11 miles of the East Coast main

Helmdon cutting, Northamptonshire, on the one time Great Central Railway. *2015.*

line near Selby were abandoned, replaced by a diversionary route in order to avoid the risk of subsidence from extended coal mining. These examples and many more have left very tangible remains in the landscape.

In many former industrial areas, abandoned railways can provide more visible remains of heavy industry such as collieries and iron and steel works than the sites themselves, which have been completely levelled. Now there is growing impetus for reopening some closed lines. The Aidrie–Bathgate, Alloa–Kincardine and other lines in central Scotland are examples where tracks have been re-laid; the south curve at Todmorden in West Yorkshire, and, in 2015, some 30 miles of the Waverley Route from Edinburgh to Galashiels and Tweedbank, the largest scheme of its kind so far, requiring new civil engineering structures and stations. Work is in progress on the 29 miles from Wolvercot, north of Oxford, to Bletchley, to be completed in 2017.

Particularly noteworthy was the creation of the 'Robin Hood Line' in 1993-8, when track was relaid or brought back into full use for 30½ miles from Nottingham to Worksop, made up of sections of three closed lines, joined together by new connections including reopening three blocked-off tunnels.

Just as viaducts are the most prominent features of working railways in the landscape, so are those on abandoned lines. A large number are listed, not only for their structural and historical value but for the positive contribution they make in a wide variety of local environments, some of which have already been noted in chapter 1. Five others can be cited as representative of the varied locations from which the railway has long since disappeared. The eight arches of Tavistock Viaduct in north Devon look down on the rooftops of the town. The fourteen arches of Smardale Gill Viaduct in east Cumbria stride majestically across a remote valley in the northern Pennines. Even more remote are two in southern Scotland: Shankend in the sparsely populated border country south of Hawick, and Big Water of Fleet, whose twenty arches, 70ft high, stand majestically in isolated Galloway moorland, the one a silent monument to an era of late nineteenth-century railway

An abutment of the lofty Belah iron trestle viaduct on the Stainmore line in Cumbria, demolished after closure in 1962. *2007.*

rivalry; the other, jointly owned by four companies, to railway collaboration. The fifth, the impressive Cefn Coed Viaduct of fifteen arches, 122ft high, curves majestically around the west side of Merthyr Tydfil in South Wales. But perhaps the most important of all is the world's oldest surviving railway viaduct at Laigh Milton on the Kilmarnock & Troon Railway of 1811 in Ayrshire, now restored. Each of these and many more make their own unique contribution to the landscape.

In quite a number of locations abandoned sections of railway have been used for road improvements, although additional land is needed because railway formations are not wide enough for a modern main road. One of the first was the western end of the Heads of the Valleys road in South Wales, utilising nearly 7 miles of the old Abergavenny–Merthyr line between Beaufort, Dowlais Top and Merthyr. The A685 road from Junction 38 on the M6 motorway at Tebay was realigned along 5 miles of the Stainmore line as far as Newbiggin-on-Lune. Also in Cumbria, the A66 now

Part of the western end of the Stainmore line was converted into a road. Gaisgill station on the right has been enlarged to form a house. 2015.

runs along much of the trackbed of the Keswick–Cockermouth line for 9 miles alongside Bassenthwaite Lake and almost to Cockermouth. Some 2½ miles of the Northampton–Peterborough line at Oundle are now occupied by the A605 road, and nearly 12 miles of the A361 trunk road across north Devon take the course of the former Tiverton–Barnstaple line.

Longer lengths of disused railway have been converted into footpaths and cycleways, many by local authorities but most notably by Sustrans, the National Cycle Route charity, and Railway Paths Ltd, both of which in total have several thousand miles of routes, substantial parts of them on old railways, including numerous bridges and viaducts. Typical examples are the Camel Trail alongside the Camel estuary in north Cornwall, the High Peak Trail on part of the old Midland main line through north Derbyshire, which includes viaducts and two tunnels, part of the Somerset & Dorset line south of Bath including Combe Down Tunnel, the Penrith–Keswick line through the spectacular Greta gorge east of Keswick and, in an urban setting, a network between Edinburgh, Leith and Granton. Similarly, a number of lengths of old railway have been designated as nature reserves or wildlife sites; for example part of the former Cardigan branch in west Wales, which also is a 14½ mile footpath.

Chapter 7

THE MODERN RAILWAY SCENE

TWENTIETH AND TWENTY-FIRST CENTURIES

By 1900 the British railway network was virtually complete. Thereafter it remained almost unchanged until nationalisation in 1948, apart from a few minor closures in the 1920s and '30s. The main changes in the railway landscape during this period were made by the reconstruction of some stations and the building of new, although in relation to the total of around 9,000 there were not that many, of which only a few made a direct impact on their surroundings, differing from their predecessors. Mainly they were in towns and cities. For instance, at the beginning of the twentieth century, Sheffield Midland and Nottingham Midland (both 1904) received impressive new frontage buildings that became city landmarks, although essentially they were late Victorian in character, while Aberdeen gained a completely new station in 1916. In 1903 the Caledonian Railway built a particularly exotic new station and pier at Wemyss Bay on the Clyde, in a striking Domestic Revival style, with a campanile-like clock tower visible from afar.

The main event in the first half of the twentieth century was the 1923 grouping of the railways when the old standard company styles finally died out and the four new large companies adopted a more eclectic approach to station architecture. The Great Western gave a classical touch to its new station at Aberystwyth in 1924, including a low clock turret; the London & North Eastern followed the fashion at Clacton in

The Great Western's 1925 station building at Newton Abbot. *1982.*

1929. The GWR went on to rebuild Newton Abbot in 1925, Newport in 1930 and Swansea in 1932, with rather bland, faintly classical but unobjectionable frontage buildings. Cardiff Central was rebuilt in 1932-35 in chunky classical Portland stone, with a small cupola in the centre of its facade. Then in 1938 the company took the plunge and rebuilt Leamington Spa in the fashionable Art Deco manner. But at all these stations the platform awnings were in a traditional style that dated back fifty years. The largest of the four railways, the London Midland & Scottish, probably did the least new work at its larger stations, although its Art Deco Queen's Hotel in Leeds became a notable city feature. It fronted the partly rebuilt former Midland station that at last was fully joined to the old North Eastern and London & North Western joint 'New' station, with the combined name Leeds City. Several smaller new stations in brick and concrete were opened in the late 1930s, such as Apsley in Hertfordshire and Lea Hall near Birmingham in 1938. The most daringly modern design was the rebuilding of Hoylake in connection with electrification of the Wirral lines in the same

year, largely in concrete in a style owing much to new work on the London Underground in outer suburbs.

The smallest of the 'Big Four', the Southern Railway, embarked on the most ambitious programme of new works and rebuilding, mainly in the south east, beginning with Margate and Ramsgate in 1926 and Hastings in 1931, all with prominent frontages containing somewhat over-sized and, by then, rather outdated classical features. Thereafter, the company went straight into contemporary modernism with some striking brick and concrete designs of which Surbiton, of 1937, is the most outstanding in what has been called 'super cinema' style. Its white concrete, very tall windows and square clock tower created a major landmark. Former competing lines in Thanet and to Greenwich were rationalised by building new connecting curves enabling former branch lines to be closed, and new lines were opened to Sutton in 1929 and Chessington South in 1938-39. Otherwise, by and large this new work was in urban locations and did not affect the broader landscape. London Transport was by far the most prolific builder of notable stations in the 'modern' style in this period, mainly on its extensions. They were designed by Charles Holden to be instantly recognisable as characteristic of the Underground, in which they succeeded admirably.

In the 1930s a number of locomotive depots were rebuilt, incorporating tall concrete coaling towers that formed new

The LMS Railway's station at Lea Hall, east of Birmingham, of 1938, represents contemporary work in brick and concrete. *1993*.

landmarks visible over a considerable distance. Only one remains complete, at Carnforth in north Lancashire, while the bare tower still stands at Immingham on south Humberside.

British Rail to Network Rail

Nationalisation in 1948 brought the beginnings of more fundamental changes. British Railways embarked on a fairly modest programme of station reconstruction. Banbury was among the first, in 1959, Harlow, Broxbourne and Manchester Oxford Road in 1960, St Helens Shaw Street and Barking in 1961, Plymouth and Coventry in 1962, Northampton in 1964, among others; all to strikingly original designs. Stafford, also in 1962, was less so; an early example of 1960s architectural 'brutalism' in concrete that has not weathered well. The platforms at Derby also were rebuilt in concrete. Flat concrete slab roofs were popular, used at Chichester in 1961, Chesterfield and Ashford in 1965, and Bletchley in the following year, all prominent buildings achieving varying degrees of effectiveness. New stations at Larbert, of 1976, Bedford, 1978, and Milton Keynes, opened in 1982, reflected – literally – the contemporary architectural fashion for large glass boxes. The new Birmingham New Street, finished in 1967, completely transformed that part of the city. After severe war damage, the old station's great arched roof on the north side was demolished and replaced by skimpy temporary awnings, followed a few years later by

Larbert station is one of a number rebuilt in the early days of British Railways. *1976.*

demolition of the rest of the place, including the hotel, to be replaced by a concrete multi-storey car park, a 21-storey block of flats and offices, and a large shopping centre, all sitting on a concrete raft over the existing narrow platforms which were dark and gloomy. 2015 saw the final completion of a second rebuilding, this time incorporating a large retail development and department store as well as offices, with striking, some might say startling, external cladding of gleaming stainless steel reflective panels, and an atrium covered by low domes looking from above like a huge blister-pack. New Street in its latest form symbolises even more emphatically the need to associate commercial development with large new stations. They are no longer imposing city landmarks in their own right. In 1972 Birmingham Snow Hill was closed and demolished, together with its hotel, and replaced by an office block. Fortunately the trackbed, which like New Street was below ground level, survived, enabling the line to be reopened with new platforms in 1987.

In 1960 the prominent Victorian frontage block at Manchester Piccadilly was replaced partly by a lower, less distinguished building followed by another employing much glass, and partly a ten-storey office block. The fine arched trainshed was retained. The opposite happened at Manchester Victoria, where the 1844 and 1901 frontage buildings, including a splendid Edwardian refreshment room, were restored, with a striking new trainshed. In 1995 the Manchester Arena was built above the through platforms, requiring demolition of an unusual iron-and-glass roof that was a lofty landmark. In 2014-15 the rather more mundane roof over the terminal and Metrolink platforms was replaced by a spectacular new one of translucent plastic panels, L-shaped in plan, on quarter-elliptical curved ribs. After its closure in 1969 Manchester Exchange station by degrees disappeared entirely. Among other city centre landmarks that disappeared during this period were Glasgow St Enoch, Edinburgh Princes Street, Cardiff Queen Street (which was rebuilt), and Nottingham Victoria, where the prominent clock tower was left as the centrepiece of a shopping centre, together with the hotel. The imposing frontage of Liverpool Exchange survived the station's closure and was very successfully converted into offices, but Central disappeared

The striking new roof at Manchester Victoria (2015), with a Metrolink tram departing. *2015.* G. Leach

altogether, although by comparison externally it was a fairly unobtrusive station. The outward appearance of a number of other stations in large towns and cities was transformed by commercial redevelopment, among them Hull, Harrogate, Southport and Walsall. In 1967 Leeds finally gained a proper frontage that incorporated tall office blocks. However, the station still lacked an entrance on the south side, an omission recently rectified by an ingenious glass-fronted pod-like structure projecting out from the viaduct over the River Aire and connected to the street by a covered walkway.

Ten London termini underwent major changes, most of all Euston which in 1961-69 was completely rebuilt, tragically losing the Doric Arch and the Great Hall in the process and receiving in their place a bland, low, flat-roofed concrete concourse building that was intended to have a hotel on top, but which never materialised. The high arched trainshed at Cannon Street, which had been severely damaged in wartime air raids, was replaced by platform awnings, and in 1963 the former hotel on the front was replaced by an office block, repeated at Holborn Viaduct and Blackfriars. Cannon Street's two landmark towers overlooking the Thames at the outer end of the station were retained, together with the tall side walls of the old trainshed. Much of London Bridge was rebuilt in 1979, and is now being rebuilt again, adjoining The Shard, Britain's tallest building. The new frontage, like the old, is still partly hidden by Borough Market Viaduct, which has been widened. Rebuilding has involved dismantling the arched roof over the terminal platforms.

In 1970, British Rail Property Board was set up to manage the whole of the railway estate. As part of its policy the site value of 'airspace' over some large central stations was realised, of which Birmingham New Street was the forerunner. Progressive changes took place at London Victoria between 1960 and 1980, latterly including building in the airspace over the platforms on the west side, where a glass-sided block replaced the ridge-and-furrow roof, rising somewhat incongruously above the original wall along Buckingham Palace Road. Broad Street was closed and demolished in 1985 to make way for a commercial development which paid for improvements at Liverpool Street next door, including more offices in place of the east-side roof, but retaining and restoring the much better west side to the extent of providing some excellent replica work.

The new Bishopsgate entrance towers at Liverpool Street station (1991) were carefully designed to match the existing building. *1992.*

Two new entrance towers that matched the original front-age completed a splendidly sympathetic modernisation. Air space development over Fenchurch Street, too, was in keeping with the retained frontage. In 1990 it was the turn of Charing Cross, where a low roof was replaced by an office block to an ingenious design clearly inspired by the profile of an arched trainshed, highly visible from the river

Terry Farrell & Co's Embankment Place development using the 'air space' over Charing Cross station (1990) is clearly inspired by the original arched roof which collapsed in 1905. *1992.*

and probably the best of London station air space development. The hotel at the front, looking out towards Trafalgar Square, was retained.

The widespread line closures in the 1960s, referred to in the previous chapter, were accompanied by the equally widespread closing of individual stations, leaving long gaps between those that remained. Station buildings were either sold for other uses, such as private houses, or were demolished, which with closed country goods yards left blank spaces, making further alterations to the traditional railway scene. A large number of small stations have been rebuilt, losing interesting or picturesque buildings that characterised the Victorian railway, in favour of small glass-sided shelters, giving them a rather bleak uniformity that has completely changed the local railway environment. Nicknamed 'bus-stop stations', because they are now unstaffed they are no longer regarded as requiring more extensive accommodation. Many larger stations that have retained their buildings have lost some or all of the platform canopies that were such a distinctive feature of the British railway station.

A late twentieth and early twenty-first century development has been the introduction of parkway stations located outside urban areas, characterised not so much by new stations set in open countryside as by their large car parks, built close to motorways or main roads with the object of attracting passengers to the railway without their having to drive into a neighbouring town. The first was Bristol Parkway at Filton, north of the city, followed by others such as Tiverton Parkway in Devon, Warwick Parkway, Buckshaw Parkway near Chorley in Lancashire and a clutch in the West Midlands conurbation. Several were existing stations, such as Didcot and Alfreton, while Tiverton was built on the site of the old Sampford Peverell station. New stations have also been built to serve airports, as at Gatwick, Prestwick, Manchester, Stansted and Heathrow, the last three on their own branch lines, although much of the Heathrow line is unseen in tunnels.

Under privatisation in 1994-96, maintenance of the railway infrastructure was divorced from the provision of train services, both passenger and freight, but after the failure of Railtrack the infrastructure, including operational control, was returned to what effectively has become public ownership under Network Rail. Despite the earlier contraction of the system it is still the fourth largest landowner in Britain, with 74,000 acres and 22,000 miles of track.

The most widespread visual change in the railway environment has been overhead line electrification, particularly in the countryside where marching catenary masts and wires mark the route of a railway far more prominently than anything in the past, when lines of poles and telegraph wires were the most visible indication, now disappeared. The current long-term programme of more electrification will continue to change the former assimilation of railways into the rural landscape into a much more emphatic feature. It began in the early 1900s on the North Eastern Railway on Teeside, the Midland Railway between Lancaster, Morecambe and Heysham, and a number of the London, Brighton & South Coast Railway's south London suburban lines. These largely experimental schemes were followed in 1931 by the overhead electrification of the Manchester South Junction & Altrincham line, but it was not until after nationalisation in 1947 that further progress was made under the 1955-67 Modernisation Plan. Today the wires extend from London to Southend, Norwich, King's Lynn and Bedford; along the West Coast route to Birmingham, Manchester, Liverpool, Glasgow and Edinburgh; the East Coast to Leeds, Edinburgh and Glasgow; on routes between these last two cities; from Paddington to Heathrow Airport; and on much of Glasgow's suburban system. Overhead electrification is set to expand considerably during the next decade, and in 2014, recognising that wiring structures can be visually intrusive, Network Rail and the Royal Institute of British Architects ran an international competition for a more aesthetically pleasing design for overline gantries, cantilevers and masts.

The adoption of high-voltage overhead wiring has meant that several hundred overline bridges and other structures required raising to give adequate clearance, making even more drastic changes to the railway scene, while many stations were rebuilt, or had platform canopies cut back or replaced to provide extra clearance, altering their appearance. Apart from total rebuilding, various ingenious bridge-raising techniques were devised aimed at minimising disruption of rail and road traffic. On the West Coast main line, for instance, numerous brick or stone-arched bridges were raised by building a concrete arch on top of the existing arch before removing it. The new arch had a flatter profile which, together with a raised parapet, often in concrete

A West Coast main line bridge at Milnthorpe, Cumbria, as reconstructed to provide additional clearance for the 1960s overhead electrification, using a concrete arch built on top of the old masonry arch which was then removed. *2014.*

blocks, destroyed the grace and symmetry of the old bridge. Even so, they are less obtrusive than many bridges entirely of concrete, as is demonstrated by their relative homogeneity compared with adjacent motorway bridges where the M6 runs alongside the West Coast main line. The East Coast main line was electrified later, when special care was taken in designing specially slender portal structures to carry the wires over listed viaducts such as Welwyn, Durham, Ouseburn at Newcastle and the Royal Border Bridge at Berwick, to make them less obtrusive. Where the railway passes through a designated Area of Outstanding Natural Beauty in Northumberland, special cylindrical lineside transformers were designed for the same purpose.

As part of the West Coast scheme a 2½ mile deviation line was built around Harecastle Hill between Stoke-on-Trent and Macclesfield on the Manchester line. It avoided three tunnels in an area of old mine workings that would have made enlargement or opening-out hazardous. The new line, which itself required a short tunnel, added an entirely new dimension to the local landscape. Further south, Rugby Trent Valley Junction was remodelled to incorporate a flyover on a concrete viaduct, while at Bletchley a new elevated Oxford–Bedford avoiding line was built, partly on pre-cast concrete beams. With stumpy legs and concrete parapets they lacked the grace of earlier viaducts. In Manchester, the Salford chord was opened in 1987 to give direct access to Piccadilly from the north.

Extensive bridge reconstruction is set to continue as electrification extends, already begun between Manchester, Liverpool and Blackpool, and in central Scotland. On the Midland main line from Bedford northward to Derby, Nottingham and Sheffield alone, it has been estimated that over 200 bridges will require rebuilding. Special attention is needed for listed structures such as the unique stone-lined cutting and bridges at Belper and Toadmoor Tunnel at Ambergate, both in Derbyshire. Electrification of the Great Western main line from London to Bristol and South Wales is under way. There the numerous listed bridges on the Bristol line make it a particularly sensitive historic railway landscape, especially through Bath, a World Heritage Site, to which special attention is being given.

Even so, demolition of some bridges on this route, and doubtless elsewhere later on, is inescapable, and a special design has been devised specifically for replacing listed bridges. Large-scale electrification is also promised on the trans-Pennine route from Manchester to Leeds, although in 2015 some uncertainty was expressed on a probable completion date.

Electrification has been accompanied by the concentration of signalling into a small number of large signal boxes, and the removal of many traditional boxes. Some of the early new ones were prominent contemporary structures. Watford Junction, Wilmslow (now demolished) and Potters Bar, for instance, led the way in being quite stylish, but as time went on others were less so. At Crewe the signalling centre was in a nondescript single-storey industrial-type building set back from the main tracks, while at Leeds it was concealed in the new station building. More recently, even more centralised signalling has proceeded rapidly throughout Britain, eventually to be concentrated in about twelve centres controlling extensive areas. The first opened in a striking new building at Ashburys, Manchester, in 2014. By the early 2020s the traditional signal box will have disappeared. A few listed examples will remain, for which another use will need to be found, leaving only the heritage railways with working examples of signal boxes and semaphore signals. Like telegraph poles, semaphores are another feature of the railway scene that soon will have disappeared. Once, many were on tall masts or, at junctions, on prominent gantries, visible from afar, but now replaced by colour lights. Semaphore signals that remain at a decreasing number of locations are nearly all on shorter posts. Eventually, colour lights in turn seem likely to disappear, replaced by in-cab signalling.

Another new railside feature is the many miles of steel security fencing that have replaced the unobtrusive traditional wooden post-and-rail or, more latterly, concrete post-and-wire. They are extending rapidly, and their close-set palings with spiked tops identify the railway in the landscape even more predominantly than overhead wires. In some places they are painted green, lessening the impact. By contrast, some parts of railways are now invisible. Cutting back lineside vegetation in steam days was

important in combating fires caused by sparks from locomotives, but then appeared to be restricted to overhanging branches that formed obstructions. Consequently, in many places the view from the carriage window was akin to passing through a linear wood. Nowadays, although parts of the railway may still be unseen in what appears to be merely a long belt of trees, vegetation is being better controlled and the diversity of wildlife respected by observing ecological good practice.

New and old fencing north of Lancaster. *2015*.

A welcome improvement in the urban railway scene has been the disappearance of large advertisement hoardings disfiguring road bridges and adjacent land, not to mention the vitreous enamel advertisement panels that defaced stations. A significant earner of revenue for the railways, they were made redundant by the coming of television and wider media advertising.

Under British Railways' Modernisation Plan ten new marshalling yards were built, occupying large acreages of land picked out by tall lighting towers. Some, like Tees at Middlesbrough and Mossend near Motherwell, were urban; others such as Kingmoor, north of Carlisle, were in virgin countryside and, in landscape terms, intrusive. Most were short-lived, closed along with older yards when wagon-load freight traffic ceased. In the ten years after 1962 nearly 500 yards were closed, varying in size, and by 1982 only 59 were still in

The southern end of Kingmoor marshalling yard, north of Carlisle, completed in 1963 under British Railways' Modernisation Plan. 2½ miles long, it proved to be a white elephant. *2015*.

use. Today some are used for other railway purposes, such as a portion of Whitemoor in Cambridgeshire and Kingmoor, the latter now only partly used but still complete with two concrete flyovers. Immediately south of it a large new traction depot replaced the old steam shed on the opposite side of the main line. Together they completely changed the landscape, as did the closure of the former yards at King's Cross, London, now only recognisable by the tall granary and some listed neighbouring buildings. Elsewhere the sites of other yards have either been sold for redevelopment or still contain a few sidings.

In 1986 British Rail began a policy of creating wildlife sites on areas of disused land, mainly rural, ranging from five acres in a triangle of lines at Syston, near Leicester; part of the Humber foreshore at Brough; 13 acres of marshy ground near Stafford – now a Site of Special Scientific Interest – a deep cutting at Goldicote near Stratford-upon-Avon, and the unused part of the former locomotive depot at Kingmoor mentioned earlier. There, interest is added by discreet notices displaying photographs of the same spot in the days of steam.

Conversely, today's environmental emphasis on rail freight has seen a number of new terminals opened at strategic locations for transhipment from container trains to road vehicles and vice versa, mostly in urban areas on existing railway land, with more planned, although Daventry near Northampton, is in open country. Yet despite present-day environmental awareness, there are still examples of former goods yards that continue to disfigure the landscape, relics of the days when some railway sites used for what was loosely called 'storage' were exempt from planning controls, resulting in their continued use for businesses like builders' merchants, scrap dealers and road haulage depots.

In 1987 the Docklands Light Railway was opened in east London, much of it on a new viaduct that visibly changed the local scene, and later it was extended to Stratford and under the Thames to Lewisham. The biggest rail event of the late twentieth century was the opening of the Channel Tunnel in 1994, followed several years later by a new high speed rail link from London across north and east Kent, now called HS1. Its course through London is nearly all in tunnel, coming into the open at Dagenham before diving under the Thames estuary to emerge amid a complex of tracks to a new exchange station at Ebbsfleet, near Dartford. Thereafter its course is mainly alongside or close to the M2 and M20 motorways to Folkestone. The complex of tracks at Ebbsfleet, Ashford and the tunnel entrance at Cheriton in landscape terms are the modern equivalent of the marshalling yards of the past. Otherwise HS1 forms a striking contrast between the minimal environmental impact of a modern double-track railway and the broad swathe of a six-lane motorway across the landscape. It also demonstrates advances in the design of concrete structures, its sleek bridges and viaducts far less intrusive than those on the motorway, particularly where both cross the Medway side by side. If and when the proposed HS2 from London to Birmingham and the north goes ahead, especially through the Chilterns where, despite the promise of lengthy sections hidden in cuttings and expensive tunnels, environmental objections have been particularly loud, the impact on the landscape will certainly be far less than that of the great gash made by the M40 motorway through the same area, accompanied by continuous traffic noise.

New railways in the twenty-first century so far have mainly been short connecting lines: for example the north curve at

The Medway
Viaduct on the
Channel Tunnel high
speed link, HS1.
2011. W. Fawcett

A train on the
Princes Risborough–
Banbury line passes
the new chord
connecting it to the
Oxford–Bletchley
line at Bicester.
2015. A.J. Aitken

Ipswich to afford direct access to Felixstowe container terminal from the Midlands; an east-west chord line and flyover at Shaftholme Junction north of Doncaster; a curve at Bicester to provide a second route from London to Oxford; a flyover and a horseshoe curve sweeping around the north of Hitchin from the East Coast main line to the Cambridge line; and a new viaduct as part of remodelled junctions west of Reading. A flying junction at Norton Bridge, on the West Coast main line north of Stafford, due for completion in 2016, is a large scheme requiring 6 miles of new line, ten new bridges, the realignment of a class B road and the diversion of a river, all of which will significantly change the local landscape. In the early 2000s the East London line was built along the west side of the former Bishopsgate goods yard, changing the appearance of Shoreditch High Street with a prominent concrete bridge.

More extensive new lines seem likely in the future, to ease congestion. Addressing the Railway Study Association in 2013 Chris Green, a former British Rail and Virgin Trains chief, predicted quadrupling of the 50 per cent of the East Coast main line between London and Leeds that still has only two tracks, quadrupling more of the Great Western main line, extending four-tracking of the Midland main line to complete it from London to Sheffield, and building relief railways to avoid congested areas. Such schemes, accompanying large-scale electrification and its associated new or modified infrastructure, are materially changing the visual effect of railways, although if they are landscaped to the same extent as HS2 their impact will be minimised.

Urban tramways have seen a remarkable resurgence. Now called Metros, the first was in Manchester in 1992, followed by

The bridge on the new East London line changed the view up Shoreditch High Street. *2015.*
A.J. Lambert

Sheffield, Birmingham, Croydon and Nottingham. Beyond the centres, where tracks are laid along the streets in traditional fashion, they have reduced landscape impact by tending to use former railway tracks or run alongside existing lines or roads, although the latest system, Edinburgh, and the new Manchester Metrolink extension, both opened in 2014 to the respective airports, have bridges and low viaducts where they run on their own individual routes.

The most prominent feature on any of the metro systems is the Queen Elizabeth II Bridge on the Tyne & Wear Metro in 1980, adding a sixth to the well-known group of Tyne bridges connecting Newcastle and Gateshead.

Several major stations have undergone transformations. Newport is now dominated by a steel-and-glass combined entrance building and footbridge gained from the platforms by prominent upswept covered escalators, contrasting strangely with the retained 1920s building and GWR canopies. A similar but far more dominant design has been completed at Reading where a virtual total rebuilding in similar style includes five new platforms, now totalling fifteen, and a much larger elevated circulating area called a passenger transfer deck spanning the

The newly rebuilt station at Reading. 2014.

station, again leaving the old listed entrance building somewhat marooned at one side and now used for other purposes. More platforms and new junctions west of the station have substantially widened the already broad band of tracks between the town and the Thames. The 1960s stations at Peterborough, St Helens and Northampton have been enlarged and rebuilt for a second time, Wakefield Westgate has at last been rebuilt many years after losing a fine entrance building and clock tower, and its handsome neighbour Kirkgate has been restored following a long period of dereliction. Glasgow Queen Street is receiving an enlarged concourse and a proper frontage appropriate to its importance, in place of the modest entrances hitherto almost hidden at each side.

Other new railway buildings, such as traction depots and repair shops, are indistinguishable from modern industrial buildings at factories and on trading estates. Traditional footbridges at a number of stations are having stairs replaced by ramps or lifts, or are otherwise adapted to assist access for the disabled. They are a welcome improvement in passenger facilities, although at some smaller stations they seem to be unnecessarily ugly and out of scale. Throughout the country traditional level-crossing gates have been replaced by lifting barriers, and doubtless will soon disappear entirely.

Bridge raising as part of gauge enhancement has taken place on the cross-country route from Doncaster to Water Orton near Birmingham, allowing European-size container traffic, and is under way from the hugely expanded east coast port of Felixstowe to the West Coast main line at Nuneaton, and from Leicester to Stoke-on-Trent, creating more changes in the railway landscape. It will do so again in the planned scheme from Southampton to the Midlands, including overhead electrification, and on the line from Peterborough to Doncaster via Spalding and Lincoln, mostly on the former Great Northern & Great Eastern Joint line.

The largest single project in civil engineering terms so far is in London, where Crossrail is due for completion in 2018. It will create a through route from east to west, joining lines at Reading in Berkshire and Shenfield in Essex, with a branch to Woolwich and Abbey Wood south of the Thames, including 13 miles of main line tunnel under central London. New surface buildings will appear, among others, at Paddington and Liverpool Street, and some interchange stations with the Underground, particularly Tottenham Court Road and Farringdon, together with a striking new station at Canary Wharf, now finished. Otherwise, at most other interchange stations, new surface buildings are mainly commercial developments, although many stations on the existing surface lines at each end of the tunnel section are being rebuilt or enlarged. Concurrently with Crossrail, the Thameslink scheme is enhancing north-south rail connections across the capital largely on existing lines but, again, with new and rebuilt stations that are changing the local railway scene.

The reopening of closed lines has already been touched on in the last chapter. Elsewhere, traffic growth on former double track lines reduced to single is now dictating restoration of the second track, as has taken place between Swindon and Kemble on the Gloucester line, on parts of the Cotswold line from Oxford to Worcester, and the Chester–Wrexham line between Saltney Junction and Rossett six new lines were opened in 1982-2014.

Taken together, all these changes are continuing to make the twenty-first century railway scene very different from its predecessors. Nevertheless, one of the most extraordinary modern railway developments has moved in the opposite direction: the emergence of the heritage railway movement. Beginning with the revival of the narrow gauge Talyllyn Railway in North Wales in 1950, there are now well over 120 heritage railways of various kinds in Great Britain, mostly operating steam locomotives on reopened lines and devoted to demonstrating bygone railway operation. Largely run by volunteers and immensely popular, they are now a major element in the tourist industry. In becoming so they have put changes in the railway landscape into reverse, restoring many lines to their earlier appearance.

Chapter 8

A CASE STUDY OF LANDSCAPE CHANGE

175 YEARS OF THE LONDON & BIRMINGHAM RAILWAY

'Its origin and establishment will constitute a memorable epoch in the history of the world' wrote the antiquary and publisher John Britton in his introduction to John C. Bourne's *Drawings of the London and Birmingham Railway*, published in 1839, a year after the completion of the line, and the best of a number of pictorial travellers' guides written in the early days of railways advising the public how to travel by train and describing what could be seen from the carriage window.

The London & Birmingham was the first trunk line from London, engineered by Robert Stephenson, aided by his able assistant Robert Benson Dockray who later became Resident Engineer for the whole line. In 1846 it became part of the London & North Western Railway. Like other main lines radiating from the capital or any other large conurbation, the London & Birmingham has undergone many changes that today would make most of it unrecognisable to its builders. Bourne's fine set of detailed lithographs and Britton's commentary, together with some unpublished wash drawings held in the National Railway Museum at York, make it possible to compare the effect of these 112 miles of railway on the 1838 landscape with the scene today.

The most obvious change has occurred on the 60 miles from Euston to Roade in Northamptonshire, where successive widenings from two tracks to four have been accompanied by major modifications to the infrastructure, to the extent that not many original structures have survived unaltered. One measure of change since Britton wrote is that in his day there were sixteen intermediate stations along the whole line, with only one, Harrow, in the first 18 miles to Watford. By the time the railways were nationalised in 1948 there were forty-three, now reduced to thirty-four. They include thirteen between Euston and Watford, indicative of the influence of railways generally on the growth of suburban London. Another measure of change is the number of branches and connecting lines that were opened and, in many cases, subsequently closed, the first being the Aylesbury Railway from Cheddington, opened in 1839 and rented by the L&BR, followed in 1845 by the company's own long cross-country line from Blisworth through Northampton to Peterborough. Others followed: from south to north, the North London Railway from Camden, the West London Railway from Willesden to Kensington and later Clapham Junction; Harrow to Stanmore; Watford to St Albans and to Rickmansworth; Leighton Buzzard to Dunstable; Bletchley to Bedford and to Banbury and Oxford; Wolverton to Newport Pagnell; the Northampton loop from Roade to Rugby; the one-time Northampton & Banbury Junction Railway from Blisworth to Banbury; Weedon to Leamington Spa; Rugby to Market Harborough and to Leamington; Coventry to Leamington and to Nuneaton. Two other companies' lines joined the London & Birmingham: the Birmingham & Derby Junction from Derby to Hampton-in-Arden in 1839, and the Midland Counties from Leicester to Rugby in 1840, both becoming part of the Midland Railway. In 1847 the Trent Valley Railway was opened from Rugby to Stafford, creating a more direct route to the north, avoiding Birmingham and now part of the West Coast main line. As a consequence of these new lines, Watford, Bletchley and Rugby grew to be important junctions with extensive layouts. Today, north of Willesden, only the St Albans, Bletchley–Bedford and Coventry to Leamington and Nuneaton branches are still open, along with the Northampton loop, although Bletchley–Oxford is in process of being restored. All

The Euston Arch. *c1920.*

these developments in varying degrees changed the landscape along the original main line.

As recorded in chapter 7, Euston has been entirely rebuilt. The cutting containing the Camden incline has six tracks instead of the four in Bourne's illustration of it under construction, although the curved retaining wall on one side is recognisable and parts of Park Street 'Tunnel', which is really a long bridge or covered way, may be original. Burrowing junctions and tunnels at the upper end dating from 1902 avoid conflicting train movements. It is interesting that Bourne's view includes fields in the distance, showing that at that time it was on the northern edge of London. For the first seven years trains were drawn up by an endless rope operated by a steam winding engine at Camden, marked by two 132ft chimneys above an underground engine and boiler house, parts of which still remain beneath the tracks and are listed. The large engine shed and goods yard that superseded them have in turn disappeared, leaving only the huge London & North Western warehouse of c1905 alongside the Regent's Canal, roughly on the site of the original railway-and-canal interchange, and the historic iron-framed locomotive roundhouse of 1847,

Bourne's view of Primrose Hill Tunnel, 1838.

now a well-known theatre and the only reminder of the early years of the railway here. A short distance beyond, the massive portal of the ¾ mile-long Primrose Hill Tunnel stands unchanged, with a second matching tunnel on the north side added when the line was widened in 1879. Unseen alongside are the two single line South Hampstead tunnels on the suburban lines, entered from the burrowing junctions at Camden. Further on, of the three Kensal Green tunnels accommodating six tracks, one is original. They were built as 'cut and cover' tunnels under Harrow Road and a corner of Kensal Green Cemetery.

Willesden became a junction in 1840 when the West London Railway was opened, followed by an east-west line crossing

Primrose Hill Tunnels today. The nearer tunnel was added in 1879, identical to the first one in the background. W. Fawcett, 2015.

over the main line. With later connecting curves, other lines and sidings, they form an extensive concentration that once included a large locomotive depot and a wagon works. By 1920 a broad band of tracks stretched onwards to Wembley. Even so, a map of 1888 shows the junction still mainly surrounded by fields. By that year the London & North Western had built a railway village of 172 houses that still stand immediately south of the station. By 1912 Willesden Junction had in effect become three separate interlinked stations. Closure of the main line platforms in 1962 reduced them to two, High Level on the West London and 'New' on the suburban lines, both now together simply known as Willesden Junction.

Beyond Willesden the widened River Brent Viaduct retains on the west side the original broad central arch and narrower side arches, although the river itself now lies in a culvert under the North Circular Road. Bourne illustrated the two viaducts at Watford, Bushey Arches and the Colne Viaduct, both having five arches that have been widened on the east side, the former with iron, later steel, plate girders. Above a retaining wall immediately north of Watford Junction station on the east side, there stands the only remaining London & Birmingham intermediate station building. The original Watford Tunnel remains as Bourne depicted it, the second tunnel of 1874 being in a separate parallel cutting. After the railway opened, Watford itself began to grow from a small town of 2,800 in 1831 to some 10,000 fifty years later, when in 1881 the LNWR, like other companies, actively encouraged even faster growth by offering free 21-year season tickets to buyers of houses above a certain figure, as they did at other stations on the line from Euston.

Nearing Apsley in Hertfordshire there are two skew bridges. The first crosses the Grand Union Canal by a broad segmental arch illustrated by Bourne, an early example of railway cast-iron bridgework but, unfortunately for its appearance, strengthened in the 1960s by encasing in concrete. The second is over the A4251 road, in brick with stone dressings, extended on the east side to take a second pair of tracks but otherwise mainly unaltered. As noted in the last chapter, Apsley station was built by the London Midland & Scottish Railway in 1938. Another skew bridge over the same road north of Hemel Hempstead is illustrated by Bourne. There the quadrupling was done by building a separate plate girder bridge alongside. Berkhamsted station of 1875 is of interest in being the last surviving LNWR standard mainly wooden station on the line, albeit with its awnings trimmed to give clearance for the overhead wires. A mile further on at Northchurch, Bourne's tunnel was quadrupled by boring two single line tunnels alongside the original one.

Tring station lost its surviving L&BR building in the late 1960s, situated at the southern end of the great Tring cutting which so impressed Britton and his contemporaries, drawn by Bourne while under construction. It is 2½ miles long and 60ft deep. In 1859 and 1876 it was widened on each side by making the steep sides even steeper, thus requiring no extra land and making it even more impressive. Between Tring and Cheddington a fine iron skewed arch illustrated by Bourne again takes the line over the Grand Union Canal at Pitstone, widened and latterly encased in concrete similar to the bridge at Nash Mills. Beyond Leighton Buzzard, additional tracks at Linslade Tunnel were laid through two new single line bores, one on each side of the L&BR tunnel. The rugged stone south portal contrasts strongly with the castellated brick turret and parapets over the north portal.

The extensive layout and junctions at Bletchley would be unrecognisable to Bourne, except for the 'bridge of great extent' at Denbigh Hall north of the station. There the railway terminated for five months in 1838 while Kilsby Tunnel was being finished. Passengers were taken by road in coaches over the intervening 35 miles to Rugby, where they reboarded trains. The bridge is acutely skewed within a rectangular plan of iron girders. They were renewed when the line was widened in 1892 and again by concrete beams in 1949, but the north side fascia beam, latticed parapet and stone abutments are original. Bletchley itself is now part of the new town of Milton Keynes which has its own station a little further north, opened in 1982 and entered through a multi-storey glass curtain-walled office block.

The new town also encompasses Wolverton, 3½ miles further on, where several features would still be recognisable to Bourne. Britton wrote that the London & Birmingham 'fixed on that point

Bourne's Pitstone canal bridge.

The same location today. *2015.*

for a *Central Depot and Station,* and to make it a magazine and manufactory of great consequence to the whole line. Here have been erected a locomotive engine house, 314ft square, provided with tender sheds, an iron foundry, smithy, boiler-yard, hooping furnaces, iron warehouse, a steam-engine for working the machinery, turning shops and lathes...and a new colony of cottages and dwellings for the workmen and their families. Hence a small town or village is established in a district previously unoccupied.' By 1844 there were over 200 houses and in 1849, two years after the L&BR had become part of the London & North Western, the number was 242. In 1854 the LNWR began to build another 187 at New Bradwell, ½ mile away, increasing the total to over 300. Thereafter Wolverton continued to grow as private developers provided more houses on land provided by the railway, built to designs specified by the company. Today only two streets of railway-type houses remain, although the greatly expanded workshops are still there on both sides of the original line, used by a variety of occupants, but to be redeveloped for housing. The oldest building is the former employees' reading room of 1839, close to the bridge of the same date over the Grand Union Canal. Widened in 1889, it still contains some original iron beams and deck plates. Towards the north end of the works, part of the bridge over Old Wolverton Road dates from 1838. In 1878-82 the main line was diverted east of the works, including a new station, leaving the old line for access only. At the southern end, where the track has now been removed, an original three-arch stone bridge spans the empty cutting. The most prominent L&BR monument is north of the town where the valley of the River Great Ouse is crossed on the Wolverton embankment and a 200yd long viaduct. Its west side is still as Bourne depicted, a graceful structure of six 60ft elliptical arches between four narrower semi-circular arches at each end. Later it was widened on the east side in a matching manner.

In another 5 miles the line enters the 65ft deep Roade Cutting, or Blisworth Cutting as it was known when Bourne made two dramatic illustrations, one showing a lofty flying arch and the other a tall three-arched bridge. Neither is there today, having been replaced when the cutting was widened in 1881-82 to take

Wolverton Viaduct, by Bourne.

two extra tracks. At the northern end they diverge from the older route to form the Northampton loop which in effect acts as a continuation of the third and fourth tracks to Rugby. As a consequence, the 20 miles of original double track line from Roade to Rugby are the least altered part of the London & Birmingham, the most obvious change being the overhead

Trees partly obscure it in 2009.

Bourne's view of Blisworth Cutting shortly after completion.

Looking today from approximately the same spot. Now it is called Roade Cutting and is four tracks wide. *2015.*

wires, some bridges that have been raised to accommodate them, and the closure of intermediate stations. Not having needed widening, many underline bridges are largely original. There is a particularly elegant, lofty bridge in local golden

ironstone over the road to Northampton, known locally as the Blisworth Arch. It stands at the point where, for the first seven years, Northampton passengers alighted to be taken along the last 5 miles by road coach.

Bourne ignores the 50yd Stowe Hill Tunnel with its bold northern portal at Weedon, but illustrates the viaduct beyond. Apart from some unsympathetic repairs, its four low arches still look much the same. Britton's account of Kilsby Tunnel, 1 mile 66yd long, is mainly devoted to the immense difficulties encountered by Robert Stephenson in building it, needing thirteen steam pumping engines to keep the workings dry and delaying the opening of the line by seven months. Bourne's drawings powerfully illustrate the construction works, including one of the two 60ft diameter ventilating shafts topped by high brick crenellated towers that are still prominent in the countryside above the tunnel. A number of narrower shafts stand between them like a line of chimneys. A well-known and particularly dramatic illustration of Bourne's depicts the interior of the tunnel at the foot of one of the wide shafts. Identical massive stone portals, 28ft high, mark the unusually tall dimensions of the tunnel. Less visible in deep cuttings, they can be seen from overbridges at both ends.

Expansion at Rugby began two years after Bourne illustrated a highly ornamental iron Gothic-arched bridge next to the first station. In 1840 the Midland Counties Railway arrived from Leicester, requiring a new station further east. Later the bridge was replaced and, after several enlargements, the station was completely rebuilt in 1885 with a large overall roof of unusual design. Long a local landmark, it in turn was removed in 2001 when more platforms were added. Strangely, part of the former Midland Railway platform still remains on the north side. As recorded in chapter 2, the railway at Rugby rapidly grew to cover a very large area, including, at the London end of the station, another prominent landmark, the Great Central Railway's massive girder bridge over the line, now gone. It stood east of complex flying junctions for the Market Harborough and Northampton lines and, built in 1948, a locomotive testing plant. Now only the main line and the Northampton loop remain, considerably reducing the presence of the railway in this area.

From Trent Valley Junction west of Rugby the London & Birmingham remains double track, although in the late 1930s the London Midland & Scottish planned to quadruple it. Some preliminary excavation was begun at Coventry station and an overbridge carrying the city's bypass road was built wide enough for four tracks; then the Second World War stopped any further work. In recent years there have been proposals to resume it. A consequence of the opening of the Trent Valley line was that the character of the original L&BR from Rugby onwards, like the Roade–Rugby section, has not changed to anything like the extent further south. Underline bridges have escaped widening and a number of the original brick or masonry arches remain. Most of the overbridges have been raised, but two tall three-arch bridges spanning deep cuttings between Rugby and Brandon still stand. Another at Adderley Park, Birmingham, was the subject of an illustration in a rival publication of 1837, T.T. Bury's *Views on the London and Birmingham Railroad*. The elegant fifteen-arch Avon Viaduct at Brandon is still much as Bourne depicted it, and the Sowe and Sherbourne viaducts on the approach to Coventry are essentially unchanged. Despite Coventry being an industrial city there are no rail-side factories on the approach from Rugby; only post-Second World War housing estates. Until the 1920s, industrial development lay on the north side of the city along the Nuneaton branch and the Coventry Avoiding Line, opened in 1914, but now closed. The rock cutting approaching the station is crossed by a fine stone flying-arch bridge, similar to the one illustrated by Bourne at Blisworth. His original Coventry station was soon replaced by a larger one, later enlarged again and then, following war damage, completely rebuilt in 1962 to a much-acclaimed design. Beyond the station the main goods yard has been replaced by new development, including a large car park.

Thereafter, in the 18 miles to Birmingham, there was only one L&BR intermediate station, Hampton-in-Arden. By the 1923 Grouping of railways there were six, two more were built by the LMS, and Birmingham International, serving the airport, was added by British Rail. Perhaps surprisingly in an area that was

Beechwood Tunnel, 1838.

dominated by car manufacturing, all nine are still open and busy, and in recent years they have been rebuilt and level crossings closed, so that in their immediate vicinities the railway now looks very different. But in the 7 miles from Tile Hill to Birmingham International, with two intermediate stations, the railway landscape is still rural. East of Berkswell, Beechwood Tunnel is just as Bourne drew it, together with an original flying-arch bridge at each end. He also illustrated the River Blythe Viaduct at Hampton-in-Arden, alongside an ancient packhorse bridge,

Bourne's viewpoint is inaccessible today, obscured by bushes and trees. This view is from the bridge. *2014.*

Bourne seems to have used artistic licence when he drew the Blythe Viaduct near Hampton-in-Arden, as the packhorse bridge on the right is out of the line of sight from his viewing point.

although compared with the same scene today he appears to have exercised a certain amount of artist's licence in his perspective. Short viaducts near Marston Green and Stechford also are much as they were in his time.

Soon after Bourne's visit the scene approaching the London & Birmingham's terminus at Curzon Street began to change utterly. Now it has changed as much again. Between the criss-crossing lines and junctions, the extensive yards, sidings and engine sheds described in chapter 4 have given way to industrial redevelopment, leaving a Freightliner depot the only

Blythe Viaduct in 2014.

Birmingham Curzon Street by Bourne.

railway presence between the main lines. The old L&BR viaduct is sandwiched between widenings on both sides, and the classical Ionic terminus building at Curzon Street, the northern counterpart to the Euston Arch, stands isolated on open ground, awaiting a new use. Proposed as the Birmingham terminus of the HS2 project, imaginative thinking could combine the very old with the very new. Whatever happens, even more radical changes are likely.

The side arches have gone, but otherwise Curzon Street is little changed. *1984.*

BIBLIOGRAPHY

Andrews, M., *The Furness Railway in and around Barrow*, 2003

Appleton, J.H., *The Geography of Communications in Great Britain*, 1962

Barman, C., *Early British Railways*, 1950

Batty, S.R., *Rail Centres: Sheffield*, 1986

Baughan, P.E., *The Chester & Holyhead Railway*, Vol 1, 1972

Biddle, G., *Great Railway Stations of Britain*, 1986

Biddle, G., *The Railway Surveyors*, 1990

Biddle, G., *Britain's Historic Railway Buildings: a Gazetteer of Structures and Sites*, 2011

Biddle, G., 'The Logistics of Railway Construction', in *Back Track*, June & July, 2009

Billson, P., *Derby and the Midland Railway*, 1996

Bourne, J.C., *Drawings of the London and Birmingham Railway*, 1839

Boynton, J., *The London & Birmingham Railway between Birmingham and Coventry*, 2004

Briggs, A., *Victorian Cities*, 1963

Brooke, D., *The Railway Navvy*, 1983

'Brunel Redivious', 'How Railways Encouraged Season Ticket Traffic', in *The Railway Magazine*, XXIV, April 1909

Cattell, J. and Falconer, K., *Swindon: the Legacy of a Railway Town*, 1995

Chaloner, W.H., *The Social & Economic Development of Crewe, 1780-1923*, 1950

Cooper, B.K., *Rail Centres: Brighton*, 1981

Cossons, N., *The B P Book of Industrial Archaeology*, 1993

Cossons, N., (ed), *England's Landscape*, 8 vols, 2006

Christiansen, R., *Rail Centres: Crewe*, 1993

Darley, P., *Camden Goods Station through time*, 2013

Dickens, Charles, *Dombey and Son*, 1846

Digby, N.J.L., *The Stations and Structures of the Midland & Great Northern Joint Railway*, Vol 1, 2014

Drake, J., *Road Book of the Grand Junction Railway*, 1837

Dyos, H.J. & Wolff, M., (eds), *The Victorian City: Images and Reality*; vol II, *Shapes on the Ground*; 12, Simmons, J., 'The Power of the Railway', 1978

Dingwall, C.H., *Ardler – a Village History, the Planned Railway Village of Washington*, 1985

Duck, R., *On the Edge; coastlines of Britain*, 2015

Emery, F., *The Oxfordshire Landscape*, 1974

English Heritage, English Landscape series, 8 vols.

Fawcett, B., *George Townsend Andrews, the Railway Architect*, 2011

Foster, R., *Birmingham New Street*; Vol I, *Background and Beginnings*, 1970

Freeman, H., *Railways in the Victorian Imagination*, 1991

Greville, M.D. & Spence, J., *Closed Passenger Lines of Great Britain, 1827-1947*, 1974

Griffith, R. & Smith, P., *The Directory of British Engine Sheds*, 2 vols, 1999 & 2000

Grosse, P., *The Railways of Carnforth, the Town and its Ironworks*, 2014

Hamilton, H., *The Industrial Revolution in Scotland*, 1966

Harper, D., *Wilts and Somerset: A Railway Landscape*, 1987.

Hoskins, W.G., *The Making of the English Landscape*, 1976

Kellett, J.R., *The Impact of Railways on Victorian Cities*, 1969

Kirby, T., 'Railways and Towns', in *How Railways Changed Britain*, 2015

Jackson, A.A., *Semi-Detached London*, 1973

Lewis, B., *Brunel's Timber Bridges and Viaducts*, 2007

Lingham, B., *The Railway Comes to Didcot*, 1992

Lindsay, M., *Portrait of Glasgow*, 1972

Lloyd, D., *The Making of English Towns*, 1992

Maggs, C., *Rail Centres: Bristol*, 1989

Miller, R.W., *London & North Western Railway Company Houses*, 2004

Morrow, B., 'The Station that Started a Village' [Lenzie], *The Scots Magazine*, April 1990

Muir, R., *The English Village*, 1981

Naismith, R.J., *The Story of Scottish Towns*, 1989

O'Dell, A.C. & Richards, P.S., *Railways and Geography*, 1971

Osborne, E.C. & W., *London & Birmingham Railway Guide*, 1840

Paxton, R., (ed), *100 Years of the Forth Bridge*, 1990

Perriam, D. & Rannishaw, D.,*Carlisle Citadel Station*, 1998

Pevsner, N., and others, *The Buildings of England, Scotland, Wales*, from 1951 and continuing

Poole, B., *Caersws: The Cambrian Railways Village*, 2013

Pryor, F., *The Making of the British Landscape*, 2010

Radford, B., *Rail Centres: Derby*, 1986

Regional History of the Railways of Great Britain, 15 vols, various authors, 1960-1989

Richards, J.M., *The National Trust Book of Bridges*, 1984

Richards, P., & Simpson, B., *A History of the London & Birmingham Railway*, Vol 1, *Euston to Bletchley*, 2004

Robbins, M., *The Railway Age*, ch 7,'Railways and the Landscape', 1962

Robbins, M., *Points and Signals*, IX 'The Railway in the British Scene', 1968

Roberts, J.E., *The Changing Face of Carnforth*, c1975

Robertson, C.J.A., *The Origin of the Scottish Railway System, 1722-1844*, 1983

Robinson, P.W., *Rail Centres: Carlisle*,1986

Shaw, I., *View of the most interesting scenery on the line of the Liverpool & Manchester Railway*, 1831

Simmons, J., *The Railway in Town and Country, 1830-1914*, 1986

Simmons, J., *The Victorian Railway*, 1991

Simmons, J., & Biddle, G., (eds), *The Oxford Companion to British Railway History*, 1999

Smith, A.J., 'The Impact of the Liverpool & Manchester Railway on a South Lancashire Township; Newton-le-Willows', in *Trans. Hist. Socy. of Lancs. & Ches.* Vol 129, 1979

South, R., *Crown, College and Railway* [Windsor], 1978

Stamp, G., *Britain's Lost Cities*, 2007

Thomas, J., *The Springburn Story*, 1979

Thompson, F.M.L., 'Towns, Industry and the Victorian Landscape', in Woodall, S.J.R., (ed), *The English Landscape, Past Present & Future*, 1985

Trinder, B., *The Making of the Industrial Landscape*, 1982

Turner, G., *Ashford: the Coming of the Railway*, 1984

Turnock, D., *Railways in the British Isles: Landscape, Land Use and Society*, 1982

van Laun, J., 'John Cooke Bourne, (1814-1860), lithographer', in *Jnl. Railway & Canal Historical Socy.* March 2014–November 2015

Villans, E.C., 'Derby: a Railway Town and Regional Centre', in *Trans. Inst. of British Geographers*, 15, 1949

Waters, L., *Rail Centres: Oxford*, 1981

Whyte, I.K., *Exploring Scotland's Historic Landscapes*, 1987

Williams, C., *Driving the Clay Cross Tunnel*, 1984

Williams, F.S., *Our Iron Roads*, 1883

Worsdall, F., *The Glasgow Tenement*, 1989

INDEX

ACKNOWLEDGEMENTS

I have to make grateful acknowledgement of the valuable comments and suggestions made by Dr Bill Fawcett, who read the initial text and took photographs; facilities for research from Lancaster University library; valuable assistance from Andrew Biddle, Richard Foster, David Lawrence, John Minnis, the late Peter Robinson, Anthony Lambert, who also took photographs, John Sanders, the late R.W. Miller, Paul Aitken; Alison Aitken for photography, the Manchester map and assistance with the index; also John Scott-Morgan, Commissioning Editor, Jodie Butterwood, and her colleagues at Pen & Sword Books Ltd.

Once again I am indebted to John R. Broughton for his skillful preparation of the illustrations for publication.

Any omissions or errors are, of course, solely my own.